Miles from Home

A True Story of the Choices that Define Us

Colleen Lanier

Wasteland Press

www.wastelandpress.net
Shelbyville, KY USA

Miles from Home: A True Story of the Choices that Define Us
by Colleen Lanier

Second Printing – April 2012
ISBN: 978-1-60047-690-7
Library of Congress Control Number: 2012933266

Printed in the U.S.A.

0   1   2   3   4   5   6   7   8   9   10

To B. My dear friend, personal compass, and a woman who rocks Garfield pajamas like no one else can. Thank you for laughing with me, crying with me, and always telling me the truth. You are an amazing woman.

NOTE TO READER

In the interest of preserving the privacy of the people involved, the name of every person in this book has been changed. The details, experiences, and conversations have been related as truthfully as possible, and any inaccuracies are unintentional.

A minimum of 20% of the author's royalties will be donated to non-profit organizations. Details can be found at www.ColleenLanier.com

PROLOGUE

It was my eighteenth birthday—I was a freshman in college. I had just gotten a letter from my best friend, Sean. He was back in Chicago, where we had gone to high school, and every time I opened my mailbox I looked for his writing. He hadn't forgotten my birthday, and as he had been born just ten days before me, he would never have an excuse for missing it. We joked about the fact that at least one of us would always remember.

I sat down and opened the envelope. An exceptional musician, he had written me a poem, the single most precious gift I was ever given:

A Creed of Solidarity,
A Verse of Explanation

Please don't think that I don't care,
or that I don't have time;
It's just sometimes I'm unaware,
I'm a prisoner of my mind.

I know it's hard when I don't respond,
for you to realize the love I feel;
But please, I pray, you understand
my love's so very real.

Through the years we learn to live,
we yearn for love and life;
We both have things we've yet to know
but youth is on our side.

Through our hearts we learn to love,
we learn to live and grow,
so please don't leave my heart behind
for the love I did not show.

And please don't think the love's not there
Or that it's gone away;
For soon, my love, we'll be as one
Soon, we'll have our day...

Sean, October 1981

I read it hundreds of times, but it would take me thirty years to really understand it. In my heart, it had always been Sean...

THE QUESTION

"So, do you want to wash your hands of this whole thing, or are you up for a road trip?"

There it was. THE question. The question I knew was coming and the one I had been wrestling with. This was a question without an easy answer. It wasn't a simple favor. It was a request for help that would require three weeks of my life, extraordinary teamwork, two thousand miles of driving and every ounce of patience, endurance, and compassion I possessed.

What I wanted to say and what I knew I would say were two different things. A few months earlier, we had ended a two-and-a-half-year relationship, and our friendship was troubled. He had been a part of my life for more than thirty years, though, and I was not the type to turn my back on a friend. It came down, quite simply, to this: it was the right thing to do.

"Yes," I said, "I'll help you."

And there it was.

I was going to travel from Seattle to Wisconsin to help my friend drive his parents across the country to their final home in an assisted living facility (ALF) in Washington State. His mother had Alzheimer's disease and would have a hard time understanding and coping with what was happening. His father had lung cancer that had metastasized to multiple sites. In spite of his declining energy and escalating levels of pain, he had chosen to make a trip across the country to see his wife settled near their son, my friend Sean.

Planes and trains had been dismissed as options, so we were about to undertake the ultimate road trip. Along the way, we were going to visit Crazy Horse in South Dakota—the one thing his father absolutely wanted to do on our "vacation." He told me before we left that he wanted this to be more of a vacation and less of an ambulance ride, but he wanted to get there conscious. That would be easier said than done.

THE HISTORY

It started in 1980, when I was a senior in high school. Sean and I were having completely different high school experiences. I got good grades, had few friends, and never felt at ease. Sean had lots of friends, didn't much care about grades, and spent his free time smoking out back. Luckily for both of us, though, we shared a love for music. He was a gifted musician who had a band and was in the show choir. I was a clarinetist of reasonable talent who loved pit orchestra and dreamed of playing on Broadway.

For the first three years of high school, our paths never really crossed. I knew who he was, but I don't remember speaking with him until senior year. That year, we ended up spending our lunch hours together in side-by-side practice rooms. He was teaching himself to play piano, and I was practicing endless scales and Mozart. I listened to him play "Color My World" over and over and over again. He listened to my scales, and our eyes met occasionally.

I don't even remember how it happened exactly, but we started talking, and a friendship was born. I think our friendship surprised people, but it became one of the most important relationships in my forty-eight years. Sean was the most talented person I had ever met, and he had the ability to make you feel special. He seemed to get along with everyone—especially the girls.

Sean was hardly a great influence in those days, though. He gave me my first drink (blackberry brandy and Sprite), and he was the first man I ever saw naked. Our timing was poor at best. I turned him down in high school because I wasn't ready for sex. He turned me down in college because he felt I was too much like a sister. We were never in the same place when it came to a relationship. We never actually dated. He was always in the back of my mind, though. Our connection could not be denied.

I knew his parents, and when I was in nursing school, I became very close with them. Sean and his parents moved to Houston when I was a sophomore in college, and when I decided to change colleges due to a change in majors, I ended up choosing the University of Texas Medical Branch (UTMB) on Galveston Island. That decision was in large part due to the fact that Sean was in Houston. We had become even closer through an active letter-writing campaign.

This was back in the 1980s when people actually wrote letters. I still have them: a history of our friendship on faded pages. The poem he wrote me for my eighteenth birthday was a permanent fixture on my wall. When I transferred to UTMB in 1983, I became his parent's house sitter. I was there many times when neither Sean nor his sister was around. His parents were like family—I called them Mom and Dad. For the purposes of this story, I will call them Joan and Henry.

Sean joined the U.S. Navy while I was in nursing school, and we started to drift apart. I became a traveling nurse and spent years crossing the country. We crossed paths in the spring of 1988. I was finishing up a thirteen-week contract at Children's Hospital of Los Angeles, and he was on leave from the navy, freshly out of rehab for alcohol abuse. He had been to Betty Ford, and our timing seemed perfect. I was moving to New Orleans for an assignment, and he wanted to visit his parents in Houston. He met me in LA, and we drove to Houston together.

That was our first road trip. It was a disaster that nearly ended our friendship. We didn't speak for over a year after I practically ran from his parent's home after dropping him off. Time healed the wounds, however, and we crossed paths again in 1990 in Washington, DC. He was learning Japanese courtesy of the U.S. Navy, and I was working at Georgetown. He had a girlfriend; I liked her very much.

It was nice to rekindle that friendship. His parents visited, and Sean and I joined them for one of those tourist dinner cruises. I still remember that dinner. Sean later told me he had found pictures of that evening while going through his parent's basement. I wished he had saved them, but they didn't make the cut. It would have been nice to add them to the photos I have from high school and college.

In the fall of 1990, I moved to North Carolina and we lost each other. There was no reason for it—we just lost track of one another. I didn't hear from him or talk to him for five years, until he surprised me by showing up at my wedding reception in December 1995. I had sent his parents an invitation, and he decided to drive up from Texas to surprise me. It was the best wedding gift I was given. He and his girlfriend stayed one night before driving back to Texas. Before they left, the four of us went out for pancakes. My husband Thomas really liked him.

For no reason at all (again), we didn't speak for the next twelve years. I sent Christmas cards to him most years and had an idea of how he was by way of his parent's Christmas letter. I never missed exchanging Christmas cards with his parents. They stopped sending Christmas cards about the time Sean and I reconnected. Providence, I suppose.

I decided to end my marriage in the fall of 2007. It was one of those save-yourself type of situations. I had sent Sean a birthday card just a few days before I admitted to myself that my marriage was irrevocably broken. He wrote back immediately, wishing me a happy birthday and telling me that his relationship of eighteen years (the same girlfriend from DC) had recently ended. I didn't write back. I don't know why.

I didn't mention my pending divorce in the Christmas card I sent him. How do you announce a failed marriage in a Christmas letter? I didn't tell many people at all, and my marriage ended with a quick divorce in January 2008. In April 2008, I wrote to Sean, telling him of my new life. He called me the day he got my letter. I answered the phone, and he said, "Do you need me to come down there?" I didn't recognize his voice. When I finally figured out it was him...WOW. It was a whole different ball game.

There was chemistry and a pull we had never had before. We wanted to see each other, and a month later, we spent five days in a cabin in Virginia. This meeting led to over a year of cross-country visits. I was in Florida, and he was outside Seattle. We spoke almost every day for sixteen months. We were together for over two months, mostly in Washington. I worked for myself and could work anywhere. I loved working from his house on the Hood Canal. It was a small, peaceful waterfront house. When we were together it felt like home, and when I asked him how long I should stay, his answer was usually "Forever."

On one of Sean's trips to Florida, my ex-husband stopped by. It was very bizarre. The last time the three of us had been together was fourteen years earlier over pancakes. Now I was dating Sean and divorced from Thomas. I watched the two of them talk, and they seemed much more at ease than me. Later that evening, Sean told me he hadn't wanted me to marry Thomas. I have asked him more than once what he meant by that, but he never explained it.

After many trips to Washington, I decided to move there from Florida to try a shared life. Sean met me in Tampa, and we drove to Washington together. He had been sober for a month and was committed to his recovery. Flashbacks to our last road trip gave us pause, but we had a wonderful trip. The picture of the two of us at the St. Louis Gateway Arch is one of my very favorites. We arrived at our tiny "new" home on August 26, 2009.

As I unpacked my possessions, I carefully hung the poem on our bedroom wall. It seemed as if Sean's words had finally come true:

For soon, my love, we'll be as one
Soon, we'll have our day…

I loved him very much and thought it was the start of the best years of my life. Unfortunately, I was wrong. When we moved in together, our relationship immediately changed. This change was not honestly addressed. We lived together very well and enjoyed each other's company. There was little to no drama and a lot of laughter. We were close enough that often one of us would say what the other was thinking. We were two peas in a pod, and it was comfortable. I would guess that everyone who knew us thought we were a happy couple.

We weren't a couple, though. We were roommates in a one-bedroom house. While that was what Sean wanted, he had not chosen to tell me, and it wasn't what I wanted or had agreed to. I was investing in a relationship, and he was interested in nothing more than friendship. We tiptoed around this difference in expectations for more than a year and a half, until I forced the conversation that led to my moving out.

Before we had that conversation, however, we made one last trip as a couple. We traveled to Wisconsin in January 2011 for his parents' sixtieth wedding anniversary. We knew his mother was declining, but we had no idea how sick his father was. On that trip, I met lots of his relatives and was embraced warmly. Everyone thought we were a couple, and I was asked more than once if we were moving to Wisconsin. It was very uncomfortable, for I knew Sean and I were in trouble.

Within a few weeks of that trip, his dad underwent a cardiac catheterization, and I traveled back for his father's aneurysm surgery. He needed open-heart surgery as well, but it was delayed due to multiple health issues. Sean started a pattern of long visits to Wisconsin with brief trips home.

I will never forget the day our relationship ended. It was February 26, 2011, exactly eighteen months after we moved into our little house. Sean was home from one of his visits to Wisconsin, and I told him there was something we needed to discuss. We had dinner and watched *Jeopardy*, one of our favorite ways to spend the evening.

After we both missed the final *Jeopardy* question, I took a steadying breath and asked the obvious question. "If we aren't going to be a couple in every sense of the word, why are we living together?"

"I love you and really like being around you. You're funny, you're smart, we get along really well, we have a lot in common, and we have fun. I can't think of anyone I would rather spend time with or live with...but there has to be chemistry."

"There *was* chemistry, Sean."

He was silent.

I knew the problem. For months, I had noticed his increasingly harsh comments about people's weight or about actresses who had gained a few pounds. I had talked with him about it on several occasions, as I've fought a life-long battle with my weight. He clearly had negative feelings about overweight people, and at some point he had decided my weight made me unacceptable as a partner. It was not something he ever said out loud.

His silence seemed to last a long time before he spoke. "I know men and women who live together as friends and they are fine with it. It works great."

"But it has to be something they agree upon, Sean. That's not what I want, and you know that. You decided you weren't attracted to me and chose not to tell me."

"I told you I needed time to figure things out. It doesn't change the way I feel about you. I like having you around, and I like living together."

"It changes the way I feel about you! How can I possibly stay here knowing the reason our relationship has changed?

"Maybe it's your issues about how you feel about yourself."

"No, it's not how I feel about myself. It is *your* issues clouding how you see me, and I can't stay knowing what you are thinking when you look at me. Sharing a bed? We need to be in separate homes."

Later that night, when we were in bed, he said, "You know who you are. I really respect that. I love you."

"I know exactly who I am, Sean."

As he fell asleep, a river of silent, hot tears streamed down my face.

I started looking for an apartment. A week later, he asked me if I was still "leaning toward moving out." He thought we could go back to being just friends. I had no idea of how that might work. Is it possible to go back to the way it used to be when you were crushed by where you ended up?

While this was going on with Sean and me, Henry was diagnosed with metastasized lung cancer. He was not a candidate for treatment, and he was given a very poor prognosis: less than six months to live.

Neither Sean nor his father thought he was going to live that long, and decisions had to be made. While one can argue the merits of many options, what made sense in this situation was for Sean to bring his mother out to Washington, where he could assume guardianship and make sure she was cared for. It takes a village, and his village was in Washington.

I thought that if Sean told his father that Joan would eventually be moving out to Washington, it would give his father the freedom to decide what he wanted to do. Staying at home was not an option, so it was a question of where he wanted to spend his final days, weeks, or months.

Hearing this idea, his father decided that he too would like to make the trip. They would move out together and settle into the assisted living facility that Sean and I had located. The move was thought of as "an adventure." One last road trip across America. I think both Sean and his father thought it would be a better way to spend his final days. It was better to be doing something instead of lying in a bed as time wound down.

Sean's parents had no idea we were trying to salvage a friendship. Henry knew we were in separate homes, but he never mentioned it to me. I honestly don't know what the rest of his family thought about us, or if they even knew I had moved out of our home before agreeing to make the trip.

I don't think Sean had any idea of how fragile our friendship was after I moved out. If he did, he gave no sign of it. I was struggling to move on while he seemed unscathed by my leaving. In many ways, it would have been easier to move out of his life completely. My heart was broken, and my pride was badly bruised. Not a good combination.

We had thirty years of history, though, and we were working through it. I had to accept that he couldn't give me the answer to the why when we had totally different concepts of the what. I knew he loved me, and I had loved him since I was sixteen. That had to be enough if we were to continue our friendship.

It would be fair to say that when I left for Wisconsin on July 21, I had packed lightly but was carrying more than a little baggage.

The Preparations

Sean and I had done much in the way of preparation before the last trip to Wisconsin. He had taken his parents to see ALFs in towns near their home in Wisconsin. They had looked at many options there, but none seemed to fit their needs.

Sean and I visited facilities in Washington after I did the research on survey scores, citations, and patient satisfaction ratings. It was a wonderful surprise when we visited a memory care unit five minutes away from our respective homes that exuded joy. It felt positive, supportive, and nurturing. We both loved it, and Sean knew he had found his mother a home.

I did the legwork in Washington while Sean did the heavy lifting in Wisconsin. In the days before my arrival, he started packing some of his parent's possessions in a U-Haul cube. I got there on a Thursday, and our plan was to leave on Sunday. During those few days, I would be a new set of eyes in sorting through their possessions.

On Friday the twenty-second, Sean took his parents out to run errands. His mom had a hair appointment, and they had an appointment at the bank. Henry had been putting off both adding Sean to their checking account and updating the power of attorney forms. As of July 2011, Joan was still the executor of Henry's estate and had his power of attorney for both financial and medical decisions. Second in line was Sean's sister Ally, who was very much on the fringes of the situation.

My father had suggested to me that I advise Sean very strongly not to get in the car for the cross-country drive without having power of attorney for both of them. We had discussed this subject several times, and Sean had pushed in his own quiet way to get this done. These documents were signed during the last few days in Wisconsin.

While they were out, I went through every drawer and every closet, looking for things that might have been hidden or put in an unusual place. With Alzheimer's comes the need for arranging and moving things around. At least it did for Joan. I found jewelry, photos, and trinkets in unusual places. They were in bathrooms, kitchen drawers, inside shoes, and under the mattress. I found things all over.

We packed what they needed or wanted to take and left everything else behind. We worked very well together to ensure that his mother would be surrounded by cherished possessions, hoping it would make the transition easier. We were leaving the house fully furnished for the estate sale his father had already arranged to take place after we left. The proceeds would help fund their care.

After several days, the cube was sealed and sent on its way to Washington. I found it puzzling and more than a little frustrating that while Henry was resistant to many of the things we wanted to take for his wife, he had us pack items as seemingly unimportant as decks of cards, old tape measures, dozens of pairs of dice, and at least one hundred old pens and pencils.

The night before the cube was picked up, I sat on the floor by his chair as he sorted through the final nightstand and dresser drawers. He handed me items and told me if it was trash, for the estate sale, or to be packed up for the trip. Items packed were called memorabilia.

As we sorted through these drawers, I was baffled by his sorting choices. He kept dozens of tie tacks for the one tie we had packed. He saved freebies from the bank, half-used notepads, and assorted rulers. Some items were left behind for the estate sale, but three full drawers yielded less than two inches of trash in a paper grocery bag.

That evening, he had Sean search for the platter from IBM he had been given in commemoration of twenty-five years with the company. It was carefully packed for the trip. His wife's beloved music box, however, was left behind. I hoped she wouldn't notice.

WORKING WITH WHAT YOU HAVE

Just before we left on our trip, I had finished two wonderful weeks of camp nursing at a camp for developmentally and/or physically disabled adults. My weeks had included a session of thirty-five- to seventy-year-olds and a session of eighteen- to thirty-four-year olds. I was responsible for the health and safety of more than forty people each day: a combination of campers, counselors, and administrative staff. I took that responsibility very seriously.

Part of my job as camp nurse was staff training. I had limited time to teach what I felt was important to the high school and college-aged counselors. I tried to leave a few essential ideas foremost in their minds. One of them was the concept of working with what you had—using what was immediately available to make a situation work.

This was relevant in adapting to Henry's rapidly declining state of health. When I arrived on Thursday, he was able to get out of his recliner with minimal assistance, and he could use a rolling walker to travel out to the garage or into his bedroom. He would sit out in his garage, perched on a bar stool to have a smoke. He got into that chair alone.

On Friday, he needed more help to get out of his recliner. They had a set of matching leather recliners that were very comfortable but not in the least bit friendly toward any level of disability. They were the kind that enveloped you when you sat down. I had to squirm forward to get out of one. Henry was having a hard time getting both in and out of the chair. It would not be going to Washington with us.

By Saturday, he was not able to get out of the recliner without total assistance. He was more comfortable sitting in one of the plastic lawn chairs on the porch or on the seat of his rolling walker.

On Saturday afternoon, he asked his son to help him stand up from the rolling walker so he could go outside. I heard Sean call me with a hint of panic in his voice. As he had tried to pull his father into a standing position, he had both heard and felt a loud "pop" from his father's right shoulder. Both he and his dad thought the shoulder might have dislocated. I did a quick check and found no obvious sign of injury. It was not broken or dislocated, but it would remain sore throughout the week. The time had come to teach Sean how to transfer and move his father safely. It was clear we would be doing more of that.

Most people don't know how to help someone in a wheelchair. If you haven't had to do it before, how would you know how to help someone move when they have difficulty supporting their own body weight? It doesn't work to push or pull them. You have to learn how to move with them while keeping them safe and supporting their body weight with your own. You have to become a combined weight.

There are all kinds of adaptive devices to help do this, but none of them were in the house. Although Sean had asked hospice to help procure a wheelchair, they had not been able to do this as Sean's dad was being discharged. We needed to work with what we had. Having just gone through every cabinet and drawer, I knew what we had: towels. Towels are wonderful tools because they are easily manipulated, have decent strength, and are washable.

It reminded me of a scenario I had posed to the camp counselors a few weeks ago. If we needed to evacuate the tents quickly, how would they do it? Sheets, sleeping bags, and items of clothing could all be used to move someone quickly. I had demonstrated how you could wrap a person much larger than yourself in a sheet and move them efficiently.

I went to their bathroom and chose a towel I had unfolded the day before when searching for hidden treasure. It was an oversized and brightly colored beach towel. It was perfect. I folded it in half lengthwise, and we wrapped it around his father's torso with the open ends in front. We used the towel to propel him up into a standing position.

It was easy, and he felt secure. There is a big difference between moving someone and moving with someone. By using the towel, our momentum, and group timing, we were able to safely move him from the chair to the bed to the car. The towel came with us, and we soon worked out a system using a second towel wrapped around the glove box handle that enabled him to position himself in the front passenger seat.

Work with what you have...

THE GOOD-BYES

The few days I was in Wisconsin were filled with drop-in visitors, errands, and phone calls. Sean and I worked well together. We shared a bedroom, and at night we would talk about the day's events and laugh at things that had happened. We also took turns guiding his mom back into her bedroom. She had a habit of turning on our bedroom light in the middle of the night or going into the guest bathroom and brushing her teeth with whatever toothbrush was handy. It was just a part of being in their home.

On Saturday night, his cousins arranged a wonderful good-bye dinner, and Sean's father had a tearful but joyous celebration. He ate a full dinner and dessert. His niece had made apple dumplings and peach pie. He loved them both. It was the last full meal he ever ate.

I knew most of the family. I got along very well with his family, and his two female cousins made sure I felt welcome. They both told me how happy they were that I was making the trip with Sean and that we would be in their prayers. When they told me they thought I was a very special person to do this for Sean, I realized they knew we had broken up. I appreciated their hugs and words of encouragement.

We left that party without their dog, Lucky. A cousin had agreed to care for him while finding him a good home, and the transfer of ownership took place that evening. I had thought that having Lucky along for the trip would offer a degree of familiarity that would be helpful for Joan, but his father had decided to leave Lucky behind. This was one of the many things I was wrong about: Joan didn't seem to notice Lucky was gone and never mentioned him again.

We added a wheelchair that evening. One of Sean's cousins had found one for us at her church. The church gave it to Henry, and it would be an absolute necessity as of the next morning. We could not have made the trip without it. Once we started our cross-country trip, he did not walk at all. A few supported steps as he got in and out of the car or in and out of the bed were all he could manage.

There were tearful good-byes, and I think everyone could tell how much this trip meant to Henry. I am glad the family in Wisconsin has that memory of him. He was excited, talkative, and seemed happy. It was really nice to see a family embrace the plan that had been regarded with much skepticism just a few weeks before. Many photographs were taken that evening, and I hope that is how he will be remembered: smiling, happy, and surrounded by loved ones.

As we pulled away from the party, we were minus a dog, but we had added the wheelchair, a prayer blanket, and a prayer shawl. They had been hand-knitted at the same church that gave us the wheelchair, and both would be well used by the end of our journey. Joan kept the shawl around her shoulders the whole trip. The blanket was passed between them.

We had no way of knowing how well his father would travel or how his mother would cope. She clearly did not know who I was and usually did not recognize that Sean was her son. She liked him, but the connection was not apparent to her. I guess she thought we were just nice people who happened to be in her home. We were hopeful that if we surrounded her with familiar items, the trip might be tolerable for her.

As far as his father went, the nurse in me had an idea of what could be expected and how to prepare. That didn't make the prospect any less daunting. He was being discharged from hospice the day we left, so until we arrived in Kitsap County, there was a medical team of two: Sean and me. I had twenty-six years of nursing in my favor, but traveling cross-country with a dying man and a woman with fairly advanced Alzheimer's was a challenge I only hoped I was up to.

Hospice had provided a comfort kit that included medications for pain, anxiety, nausea, and respiratory distress. I had a blood pressure machine and stethoscope, along with his glucometer and testing supplies. I had packaged two weeks' worth of medication for both of them. I had wipes, disposable pads, and a bag specifically for "accidents" along the way. I was reasonably prepared.

SUNDAY, JULY 24

On Sunday morning, Sean and I ran around and tried to occupy his mother's attention. She was agitated by the changes within the house. Things were not where they used to be, and the house felt chaotic and messy. After breakfast, she wiped the dirty dishes with a napkin and put them back in the cabinets. It was something she had been doing for a while, much to Henry's dismay. While I had always diverted these dishes into the dishwasher after she left the kitchen, I just let it go on this particular morning.

It was a difficult morning for all of us. I worked on making sure the car was packed with everything we might need, while Sean focused on making sure nothing important was left behind. Henry was reluctantly handing over the financial oversight of his brother's money to a niece. The issue had been headed to court, and Henry waited until the very last minute to let the niece know that he was going to give the responsibility to her. The brother's mail had already been forwarded to Sean's house in Washington. It was one more thing Sean would have to take care of.

We were finally ready to head out. Sean had been discussing our upcoming trip with his mom for days, and she seemed to be happy with the idea of going on a vacation. We said it was time to get our vacation started and it was really easy to get her into the car. Both Sean and I did a last-second walk-through. The house looked like they still lived there, and it felt odd to be leaving it that way.

Right before we pulled out of the driveway, Henry sent me back in the house to collect all of the land-based phones. They would never have a landline again, but that was the last thing loaded before we left. I resisted the urge to take her music box and will always wish I had picked it up for her. Henry and Joan were in the car, and Sean and I stood by the trunk as I found space for the telephones.

"So, you think we're ready, Beanie?" Sean had given me the nickname of Beanie the year before. He was the only one who called me that. I liked it.

"As ready as we can be, I think. How are you feeling?"

"Ready to get going. I want to get home."

"Only two thousand miles to go, Sean. Piece of cake, right?"

"I'll be so happy to be home."

We hugged—something we did often. Sean gave stellar hugs, and as I was a full foot shorter than him, his chin rested comfortably on the top of my head. It was a long hug, and I think we were both trying to summon our strength for what was to come.

When we pulled out at around 11:30 a.m., Joan did not know it was for the last time. The "For Rent" sign in the yard puzzled her, as it had on many occasions in the past few weeks. She read it over and over, which was something she did frequently. She liked to read signs.

We made one last stop before leaving town. Sean's uncle lived in a nearby retirement home, and Sean's dad wanted say good-bye to his brother. This brother had been in a nursing home for years and, ironically, would outlive all of his siblings. It was his finances that were the subject of conflict. His brother was wheeled to the side of the car because Sean's dad was not feeling well enough to get out.

The brother didn't really understand when Henry said he had cancer and had two weeks left to live. That two week number surprised me—I didn't know where it came from. He said he wasn't getting better but was getting worse and was sorry to leave him. After a few minutes, Sean wheeled his uncle back into the building. It was hot outside and watching this good-bye was very sad. It was 11:57 a.m. when we hit the trail for Washington.

A SUNDAY DRIVE

The first day of our trip followed a winding path through western Wisconsin. Sean had vacationed there as a child, and his father's parents had lived there. It was a beautiful day, and the drive was really pretty as we passed cute little towns, rivers, and open spaces. I had never been through this part of the state. Our goal was to get to La Crosse and stay there, getting a good night's sleep for the following day.

As we drove through little towns, Sean and his dad reminisced about the past. Joan didn't participate in those discussions—she just looked out the window and read the billboards and signs. I don't know if any of it looked familiar to her, but she seemed to enjoy the drive. We were "taking a trip," and she liked being out of the house, I think. As her Alzheimer's had progressed and Henry had gotten weaker, her world had become quite small.

Most of her time was spent entertaining herself in their condo or watching whatever channel he had chosen. Maybe it is a guy thing, but Henry kept a very firm grip on that remote. He watched CNN, *Matlock*, and the *Golden Girls* at ear-deafening volumes. It didn't matter what anyone else wanted to watch, or even if people were already watching something else. He changed the channel whenever he wanted to and slept with the remote in his hand. At night, the volume kept me awake. I had tiptoed up to his chair and turned down the volume many times. I knew he had awakened when the volume went back up.

Joan had a few favorite things that were frequently moved around the house. Sean said she thought they were moving one day and had piled some things on the foyer table. It was a blessing, he said, as it told him what was important to her. There was an embroidered table runner, a photo album with very old photos in it, and an angel. She loved angels, and we had packed many in that cube.

There was one other thing that she really loved: Ronald Reagan. She just loved him. During one of his trips to Wisconsin, Sean told me about a magazine with Reagan on the cover that she was attached to. She would put it on the couch as if he was a visitor. I didn't remember that magazine from my two visits out there earlier that year, and I do not know where it came from. She certainly loved his smile, though, and it was the first thing designated as a back-seat necessity.

Before traveling to their house, I had done a little shopping and found three small picture books: one of dogs, one of babies, and one of mothers and children. She really liked pictures of children. It made her smile to look at them. One of the packages of baby wipes had a drawing of a baby on it, and she would hold it sometimes while sitting on the toilet. When the time came to pack the car, I had filled a Walmart bag with her photo album, the picture books, a pad of paper, and Ronald Reagan.

On this first day of the trip, she held onto Ronald and talked about him visiting her dad. She said he was such a nice man, and with a wicked little smile, she said she would "like to have him for a day." I was shocked when she said that. She would repeat that sentiment many times. She particularly loved his smile. While she didn't recognize Nancy Reagan, she thought Nancy looked like a very sweet lady.

We stopped for gas, and I took Joan into the bathroom. I had learned a valuable lesson several months earlier when she had locked herself into a stall and could not get out. It was stressful for both of us as I failed miserably in all attempts to calm her down. I had to squirm under the partition to let her out, and I did not want to try that again. If there were multiple stalls, I went in with her or I held the door open.

Going to the bathroom was a group endeavor, as I had to provide varying levels of prompting, assistance, or total help. I would use the bathroom while she washed her hands, always rushing so I could be done before she started wandering. A little on the shy side, I took comfort in the fact that she would not remember our "group pees." Privacy was not an option during this trip.

We had a little difficulty getting Joan back in the car as she was not convinced it was the right vehicle. It gave Henry time to finish his cigarette before we were all settled in and buckled up.

CRAZY FRANKS

As we traveled a little further down the road, Henry started talking about Crazy Franks, a place with a little bit of everything where he had shopped years before, always finding something he needed. He wanted us to stop there. We found it in its new building in Readstown, Wisconsin. Their slogan was "50,000 items selling for peanuts." This would be our second stop of the day. Henry stayed outside in the car to have a smoke while Sean, Joan, and I headed inside.

Joan and I started with a group trip to the bathroom, and then we walked around. There truly was a little of everything: vintage clothing, birdhouses, collectibles, food, tools, and housewares. She liked things that were glittery or shiny, and we picked up many items as we walked around. When I stopped to look at pillows, she started loading up on them. She had at least five when she started down the aisle. I called her name, and when she turned around, there was no face—just a big pile of pillows with legs.

I bought an overstuffed pillow for $4.44, a wedge pillow for $3.98, and a blanket for $2.00. It had been electric at one point and had wires running through it. There was no way to plug it in, thus the bargain price. It was blue on one side and tan on the other. It was tacky, but Joan had stated she was cold on several occasions, and I thought it would come in handy. She was wrapped up in that $2 blanket for most of the trip. If the blue side showed, she was fine, but if the tan side was visible she thought it was icky.

When we got to the checkout counter, Joan started picking at stray pieces of paper, rearranging the "impulse" items at the register and talking in a way I could not follow. I had no idea what we were talking about. The cashier just smiled, patted my hand, and said, "I know all about it, honey. My mom too. God bless you both." Joan gave her a big smile and told her she was a good girl.

Sean found a free popcorn machine and took a bag out to the car. Once I got Joan buckled in, I went back for a second bag. Joan quickly polished off one bag and started on the next. When it was about halfway eaten, she turned down the edges and passed it up to her husband. He had eaten next to nothing that day—his appetite had been steadily declining, and getting him to eat was a challenge. He ate that popcorn, though. He said it hit the spot. It would be the bulk of his calories that day. All in all, our $10 stop at Crazy Franks was priceless.

THE LAST NIGHT OF SLEEP

We made it to La Crosse that afternoon and continued into Minnesota. We drove a total of 293 miles and ended up in the city of Albert Lea. We checked into a very nice hotel with friendly people who worked with us to provide a handicapped room for Joan and Henry and a room with an adjoining wall for us. As we pulled into the hotel, Henry asked for his wallet. He handed Sean a credit card. After we checked in, the credit card went back in his wallet to be stored in the armrest compartment.

We got Henry settled into bed, and the three of us went to Applebee's for dinner. We were tired but happy to finally be on the road. Joan and I each had a glass of wine, and we clinked "Cheers!" to a good trip. Sean joined in with soda water and lime. This restaurant had a Disney theme, and Joan really liked the pictures on the walls. The hostess had a pink flower in her hair, and it was admired every time she walked by.

It was a nice dinner, and we were comfortable letting Henry sleep back at the hotel. We had a nice conversation and enjoyed each other's company. Sean and I were able to find the humor in his mom's dismissal of silverware as necessary implements.

Everything was potentially finger food to her. Broccoli, steak…you name it. You had to laugh…when she was done chewing a piece of steak, she just spit it on top of her mashed potatoes and smiled. It was so unlike the gentle and well-mannered Joan I had known. We relaxed, had a very nice dinner, and got back to the hotel to find Henry sleeping peacefully. We brought him an Arby's sandwich, as that had sounded good to him. He ate about one-third of it later that evening.

I repacked luggage, trying to decrease how much stuff we needed to bring in with us every night. Leaving a suitcase in the room with Joan resulted in multiple clothing changes. She would put on her clothes or Henry's. She often put on two or three layers of clothing. If she saw her shoes, she would put them on—often immediately after she took them off. Layering clothing was something she frequently did. I guess the more outfits the better—there must have been some comfort in it.

His parents settled in for the night. His dad had the room phone in reach, his cell phone next to him, and our wall was about ten feet away. We told him that if he needed us, he could just throw his shoe at the wall, and we would come running. He thought that was funny. We were all asleep pretty quickly that night and slept through until early the next morning. It was the last decent night's sleep I had for quite a while.

THE BEGINNING OF THE END

In the morning, I helped Joan get cleaned up and dressed. This was the first morning Henry asked for morphine. We had the concentrated liquid, which worked quickly before getting to the stomach—it went right under his tongue. Sean wheeled his father out for a smoke and then settled him at a table for the hot breakfast in the lobby.

I was busy helping Joan take a shower. She no longer thought of showering on her own, and it was often a struggle to get her into her bathroom at home. There had been a home health aide coming out to their home to shower her for the past several months, and since we were on the road, that task fell to me. I had packed lotions and scented shampoos I hoped she would like, and I tried to make showering fun. We did pretty well that morning and were soon ready for breakfast.

As Sean came back into the room to start loading the bags, the phone rang, stopped, and rang again. It was the front desk telling us that Henry wasn't feeling well and had started vomiting.

Sean ran to help his father while I took his mom to the lobby for breakfast. We took turns watching his mom, who was thankfully unaware of her husband's distress. Henry was outside by the car, ready to go. Neither Sean nor I ate as we tried to get everything back in the car and get moving. I grabbed coffee for both of us and we pulled out at 8:30 a.m.

As we got underway, Sean's father mentioned that he had needed help the night before when he wanted to use the bathroom and thought that "if the girls were up for it" maybe we could all stay in one room from now on: he and Sean in one bed and Joan and I in the other.

Sean and I locked eyes in the rearview mirror. It was interesting this subject came up so quickly; there had been a few conditions I set when I agreed to make this trip and having two rooms was one of them.

THE TERMS

Before I agreed to this trip, Sean and I had talked about the possibility of my helping him. I had been very vocal with both he and his father that I thought a road trip was a really bad idea. One night when Sean was at my house, his father called to ask if I was "on board." Sean told him I thought the whole thing was a terrible idea but that he thought I was up for it. I had not said yes yet and had not known that my taking the trip had already been discussed with his father.

I was the one who had researched and priced traveling by train. I had been in favor of a train because bathrooms would always be accessible, and you could sleep whenever you wanted to. The three of them could have traveled in a handicapped-accessible compartment. I had offered to drive their car to Washington. That suggestion had been vetoed because Henry said he would be asleep when they went through the areas he wanted to see. He wanted to go to Crazy Horse, so it was going to be a drive.

I told Sean there were a few non-negotiable terms if I agreed to make the trip. The most important thing was that I had to be back in Washington for an appointment at 9:00 a.m. on Monday, August 1. That was an absolute end-date for me. It was eleven days from the time I arrived in Wisconsin to the time I absolutely had to be back.

When we discussed the drive, Sean thought a goal of three hundred miles a day would be good. It was about two thousand miles, which meant we would be on the road for seven days and six nights if all went well. We thought we would get to Washington on Saturday the thirtieth. That gave me a one-day buffer. We had discussed that if we weren't close, I might have to fly back from wherever we were in order to meet my deadline.

The second condition was that we shared the driving. Being in the backseat is usually boring, but being in the backseat on this trip would mean being the primary source of interaction with his mom.

Confusion, having the same conversation dozens of times, and trying to keep her seat belt on were all a part of the back-seat responsibilities. While there were certainly moments of laughter and fun, it was often a challenge.

The third condition was that we did not share a room with his parents. I had no problem sharing a room with Sean. We had shared a home together, so that was nothing new. I am a person who likes privacy, however, and sharing one room was just too much: too many people, too little privacy, and too many people sharing one bathroom when hygiene was often less than ideal.

Sean agreed that my three conditions were reasonable. However, a fourth issue arose after I arrived that I did not know I would be facing. Had I known it would be a part of the deal, I never would have agreed to make the trip. It was an absolute deal-breaker for me.

I really dislike smoking. I hate it, actually. It makes my eyes water, my nose itch, and usually gives me a headache. I can tell if someone has been in a room with a smoker. My grandfather smoked, and whenever he mailed a package to us, we were hit with the smell of Lucky Strikes as soon as the box was opened. My mother shared my intense dislike of smoking—or perhaps she passed it on to me.

In the spirit of full disclosure, I should admit that I smoked for a week the summer after I graduated from high school. Well, I pretended to smoke. I never quite figured out the inhalation aspect and mainly held it in my mouth and tried to exhale as coolly as possible. I started smoking because I had a wicked crush on the marine recruiter who worked across the street from the health food restaurant where I was working. Neither the crush nor the smoking lasted very long, and that was the end of my habit.

Sean used to smoke. I will give him credit both for quitting and for being a very considerate smoker. He never smoked in his own home, never smoked in mine, and stood far away from me when he did light up. Even in his own truck, he rarely smoked when I was in it, and never with the windows up.

Sean's father was a smoker, and the diagnoses of triple-vessel coronary disease, aortic stenosis, an abdominal aortic aneurysm, and end-stage metastatic lung cancer did not lessen his desire. His primary physical activity in the last weeks of his life was first walking, then using a walker, and finally being helped in his walker as he headed out to his deck or the garage to smoke. It was baffling to me, but clearly his right and his choice. His wife never liked that he smoked, and in the more than thirty years I knew him, he had always smoked outside.

This had changed in the last few weeks. He began smoking in the car. When Sean picked me up at the Milwaukee airport, I had a headache within fifteen minutes. Every time I sat in the car, I got a headache. I attributed the smell to the car sitting in the smoke-laden garage with the windows down. One of Henry's relatives brought an ashtray that fit in the car's drink holder, and when I saw it, I asked Sean if his father was now smoking in the car. Sean's response was very matter-of-fact: "You can count on it." I was furious.

This would be the subject of my first call to my parents. They knew about my trip and some of the details about my split with Sean. They had recently visited me in Washington, and Sean had spent some time with them. My father and Sean discussed the possible drive and some of the things Sean could expect to deal with as he became more involved in his parent's care.

When discussing the drive and my serious reservations about the undertaking, Sean never mentioned to my father that he had asked me to join him. I wondered why he left that part out. So did my father. At the time Sean and I were discussing the trip, the thought was that I would be needed primarily to help with his mother. Her doctor had said Joan could make the trip if a there was a female along to help take her to the bathroom, help her shower, etc.

This was less than a month before the trip began, and the primary concern was taking his mom to the bathroom while on the road. We agreed that the trip would be tiring for his father, but at that point, his ability to make it was not a concern. Henry's decline just a few weeks later was precipitous and way ahead of the timeline his doctors had given him.

Back to the smoking issue…the four of us were only together in the car once before we hit the road. That was when we drove to the good-bye party on Saturday night. A few minutes into the drive, his father lit a cigarette, and smoke blew into my face. I developed an immediate headache. Rolling down the window didn't help, and when Henry put his window down in response to mine being lowered, all of the smoke shot into my face. By the time I got to the party, my head was pounding and I was in a very bad mood.

This window war was repeated on the way home from the party. As I considered this new problem, I weighed my options and considered flying home. Sean asked what was wrong. I had been quiet since getting back to their house. I didn't feel well, I was angry about the smoking, and I was very concerned about the rapid deterioration I had seen in his father in the three days I had been there.

I told Sean that if he had told me his father was smoking in the car, I would not have come, and the fact that someone dying of lung cancer had no qualms about blowing his smoke in the faces of the people trying to make his last wish come true really bothered me. Sean said I should talk to his father about that. I gave him a long look and continued packing my bag. He left the room, and I considered my options. A few minutes later, he came back into the room saying that his father had agreed not to smoke in the car, as I was "too important."

All of us should have been too important, but I was glad Sean had done this for me and that Henry had recognized my right to not be exposed to secondhand smoke. As his father became too weak to get out of the car, he rolled down his window and smoked while we were stopped. I could understand that, and hopefully there were no hard feelings.

MONDAY, JULY 25

We drove across Minnesota that morning. Henry was sleeping most of the time and not eating anything. I continued to offer drinks, fruit, and a wide variety of snacks. I had filled a large Tupperware container with granola bars, cookies, crackers, cereal bars, and fruit of all kinds. The cooler was full of diced fruit, Jell-O, sugar-free protein drinks, and assorted sodas and water.

This container sat under the cooler between Joan and me. We were packed in the backseat pretty tightly, but we had access to everything we needed. Opening the food box so Joan could go shopping was an effective distraction when she got restless or started to get agitated. Her doctor had prescribed a low-dose anti-anxiety medication in case of trip-related agitation, but we tried to use it only at bedtime to help her settle in. We worked together to try to keep her engaged in conversation or sightseeing.

There was a lot to look at out the windows as we crossed the state. Minnesota was onboard with wind-based energy, and there were hundreds of windmills. I liked watching them circle, and Joan did as well. When I told her I thought it would be fun to take a ride on one of them, she thought it was pretty funny and said, "Whoa, mister. You better watch out."

There were lots and lots of billboards to read as well. I figured out pretty quickly that her ability to read was a good indicator of her comfort level. On good days, she read quite well. When she was agitated, frustrated, or ill at ease, she stumbled on the words. It let me know that I needed to do something different.

Monday, July 25, was an important day for Sean, and one I was very happy to see. It marked two years of sobriety. It was the first milestone day that I had been able to share with him. We had been apart for both his six-month and one-year achievements. I had seen his tremendous progress as he took control of his life, finances, and responsibilities. I watched my friend come back from the edge and was so very proud of him.

I knew Sean well enough to know he would not say anything about this day, so I did. I announced it was a very special day and that Sean was celebrating his second birthday. That is what it is called in AA, and Sean was active in the AA community.

An avid card-shopper, it gave me more opportunities to search for the perfect card as his friends celebrated birthdays. On Sean's first birthday, I had bought bags of jelly beans, calculating how many drinks he had NOT had during the past year. I gave him one jelly bean for each drink not taken. I had a very good idea of what that number would be and hoped the volume of candy would illustrate the magnitude of his accomplishment. He still has one of those bags in his house.

His father was supportive, congratulating him on "the day he had waited a long time for." He said it was a good thing and that it made him happy. Then, oddly, he thanked me for the part I had played in it. That brought tears to my eyes, for in many ways Sean's sobriety had cut me out of his life. The anonymity of AA means that things must be kept away from "significant others" who are not part of that world. Time spent in AA is time not spent with the people at home.

On a few occasions, Sean said the topic of discussion at a meeting was taking care of the home front in addition to focusing on recovery. It was not something he always took to heart, though, and it caused some hard feelings. While he would drop everything he was doing to answer a call for help from someone within AA, he would not do the same for me.

I felt that I had taken a backseat to his recovery and the recovery movement more often than I should have. He would spend a day helping a fellow AA member, but favors I asked for were often at the bottom of his list. I had brought that to his attention, but it was not something we had resolved. I still do not understand it.

I do not in any way mean to imply that I wished he had not found AA or recovery. I would not have a friend at all if it weren't for his decision to choose sobriety. I am simply stating that recovery comes with a price to those around the person who do not share an addiction. The price I paid was that, while we were together, I was never one of his top two priorities. That hurt when we were together, and it still hurts now.

I did not have an instrumental role in his sobriety. That was all Sean. I like to think that I gave him a safe place to land. He was able to do what he needed to do while living in an atmosphere of calm support. He knew he could lean on me, and I would not let him down. If nothing else, I am dependable. I was overcome with a case of the "if onlys" when Henry thanked me for helping his son. Some wounds heal slower than others…

Joan and I resumed a conversation about the passing billboards. It was getting close to noon, and we asked Henry if anything sounded appealing. Arbys won again, and we pulled into the parking lot. We ended up parking way in the back, under shade. Henry was not planning to get out of the car, but he wanted us to go in for lunch. It gave him privacy to smoke, and maybe he wanted some time alone.

Joan, Sean, and I went in and sat down. Sean and I ate pretty quickly. It was hot outside, and we were thinking about getting back to the car. This was not one of Joan's better days, though, and she could not get going on her sandwich. The fries were eaten, but she was stuck on adding sauces to the sandwich.

That happened pretty frequently. She would add condiments, move things around, and then repeat the process. It could take several rounds of condiments before she could start actually eating. Removing them didn't help, because she would look for them. You just had to work with her until she got started. Sean had already finished and gone outside to check on his father before she took her first bite. That bite was followed by another round of sauces. I realized we were asking too much of her.

Every place we took her was unfamiliar. She had no frame of reference other than us, and she didn't really know who we were. She kept asking about "Daddy." Oftentimes, we think she saw her husband as her father. Most times she spoke of her parents as if they were alive. She did not understand that Henry was going to remain out in the car and wanted to wait for him.

When we were finally ready to go, she started cleaning the table and picking up crumbs from the floor. She wanted to collect those plastic advertising placards from surrounding tables, and some people were less than gracious about it. I ended up practically dragging her to the ladies' room to wash her hands. Not one of our better meals.

I realized we needed to change our strategy. Joan was most comfortable in the car—she almost always knew it was her car. We did not take her into another restaurant during the trip. We tried to make her world as uncomplicated as we could. She was most comfortable when it was just the four of us with minimal distractions. We were making adjustments on a very steep learning curve.

Ronald Reagan helped her settle into the backseat. It was my turn to drive and Sean's first foray into the backseat. He spent time looking through the photo album. It was really very interesting. Joan recognized every picture of her mom and dad, but she did not recognize herself or her husband.

She never identified pictures of her children, but she would smile and tell me how cute they were. I would tell her how cute I thought her son was. She did not know he was in the car. If you asked her to identify someone in a photo and she did not recognize the person, she would smile and say, "Yup, yup, yup." It helped to then point to her mother's photo and ask her a question to which she knew the answer. It made her more at ease.

The afternoon passed quietly. Two rest stops and one fill-up later, we were approaching the Black Hills. We had been reading dozens of billboards for Wall Drug and had hoped to make it that far. It was not to be, though, for when Henry asked about our progress in terms of miles it meant he was ready to stop. When asked if we should look for a hotel, he would say something like "when we see a good one." That meant as soon as possible. We made it to mile marker 150 and ended up in Kadoka, South Dakota.

TABLE FOR THREE

We checked into an inn. It was a rather sad motel in a sad little strip of motels. The area was dusty and run-down. The front desk clerk was very friendly, however, and let us look at the rooms before renting them. Sean and I agreed that adjoining rooms were more important than handicapped accessible and decided we could make it work. We went out to the car to tell Henry it would be fine.

"Well, you'll need my credit card to pay for the room. Hand me my wallet, will you, Sean? I'll give you the card and then bring it back to me."

Sean retrieved the wallet from the compartment between the front seats. "I'll bring it right back, Dad."

"Just give it back so I can put it in my wallet once you pay for the rooms. Maybe you should take my AARP card, too."

"I'll be back in a minute."

Sean paid for the rooms and came back to the car. Henry held out his hand without saying a word, and Sean gave him the credit card. Once Henry had put the card back in his wallet, he handed it to Sean to store in the compartment.

This scenario would be repeated every time we stopped for gas or checked into a hotel. Henry hung on to control of his money very tightly. I thought it must have made Sean feel like a child asking daddy for a credit card, but he handled it with grace. Sean was wonderful with his father.

We cranked the wall A/C units on and got to work. Henry sat in the parking lot and had a cigarette. I have an image of him in the wheelchair parked next to a big planter of wilting flowers as he smoked. He did not look good. Each day was taking a little more out of him, and in my head I had already started recalculating how quickly we could get to Washington.

We had adjoining rooms, and the door between them stayed open. After getting Henry comfortably settled into his bed, Sean and

I unloaded the car. As I entered our room through Joan and Henry's side, I found Joan in our room looking around. She gave me a huge smile and wrapped her arms around me, saying, "I'm so glad to see you again." We hugged for a long time. It was touching—she may not have known who I was, but she recognized me and was happy to see me. Sean heard it from the other room, and I could see him smile.

A few minutes later, Henry vomited, and it got on his clothes and the bed linens. We called housekeeping to bring us more sheets, and in the interim I used the towels to create a dry bed. The trash can was nicknamed "my puke bucket."

"Henry, I'm sure you already know this, but I don't think your body can tolerate the smoking."

"What?"

"Every time you have thrown up, it has been right after you had a smoke. I think your body is trying to say no to cigarettes."

"Well, I've been thinking about quitting."

Sean spoke up right away. "Dad, we can get some patches or nicotine gum."

"That's just substituting one addiction for another," he said.

I had heard that several times before.

"I guess I'll just quit. It's probably time."

There was no question of leaving Henry alone to have dinner. There were two things to be done, and both of us were tired. We needed to watch Henry and try to have a normal dinner with Joan. Neither option was relaxing. There is strength in numbers, though, so we opted for dinner in the room. There was a restaurant in the parking lot, and I went on a field trip to get a menu. Sean's brief respite was to go place the order and wait for our dinners. While he was gone, I set up a table for three in our room.

It was a sad little dinner. The food was okay, the room was okay, and the weather was turning stormy. There was a nice little storm that blew through, and it gave us something to look at out the window. Sean got a grilled cheese for his father as it had sounded good to him the day before. Henry ate about one quarter of it. That would be, for all practical purposes, his last "meal" of any substance. One quarter of a lukewarm grilled cheese sandwich.

I helped Joan into her nightgown, and we turned on the television in her room. Henry was sleeping on and off. We put the remote control by his hand in case he wanted to crank up the volume. Once they were settled, I put on my PJs. For a forty-eight-year-old woman, I have juvenile pajamas. I had bought them for camp, where it was not uncommon for me to head out to the tents at night, so everyone got to see them. I had packed stars, owls, and Mickey Mouse pajamas for the trip, and Joan seemed to like them.

Sean and I were ready to go to bed.

"Which bed would you like?" I asked.

"Doesn't matter."

"Well, do you want to be closer to the bathroom or the AC?"

"I think you will probably hear them better than me, so maybe you should be closest to their door." It was also closer to the AC, which was fine with me.

There was no doubt I would hear his parents if they called. Sean could sleep through sounds, movement, and even someone calling his name. I both envied and was frustrated by this ability. It was not something I could do. I have slept with one eye open for as long as I can remember.

DEGREES OF SLEEP

There are many ways to sleep. Some are far more restful than others. Sean slept like a forty-seven-year-old man without children. He could sleep through almost anything once he fell asleep. Getting to sleep was sometimes problematic, but once he was down, he stayed down. It is a sleep most women can only long for.

I, on the other hand, slept like a camp nurse. I think that would be second only to a mother with a sick child. At camp, my room had been on the lower level of a lodge with a creaky staircase. I would hear the counselors when they hit the first step. By the time they got to my door, I was already up and opening it. As a child, my sister and I slept on bunk beds. She had asthma, and I would wake my parents when her breathing changed.

I heard everything: Sean sleeping, sheets rustling, cars pulling into the parking lot, and every position change by both Joan and Henry. I was awake every time Joan started wandering. This particular night, Joan was up every two hours. She was in our room three times and used our bathroom once.

Sean slept through all of it. Each time she came in, I would lead her back into her room and guide her to bed. When Henry got up to use the urinal, he called for Sean. While Henry was still able to sit up, he needed help with the details. I had to go over and shake Sean to wake him up.

Sean helped his father and was back asleep in less than a minute. Thirty minutes later, I was still awake and wondering how he did it. It was the first but not the last time I was tempted to throw a pillow at him. Or poke him with a really big stick…

Sleep deprivation became a big part of this journey, but on this night in South Dakota, it was just a lousy night's sleep erased by the big cup of coffee Sean gave me as soon as we were both awake. He was excellent at keeping us supplied with coffee at every hotel. He even helped me squirrel away Splenda so I never ran out. I have been an artificial sweetener kleptomaniac since I was sixteen. I started with the pink packets and never stopped. I don't know if that qualifies as an addiction but I have absolutely no intention of stopping.

TUESDAY, JULY 26

Tuesday morning was the start of what we hoped would be a big day. Henry wanted to see Crazy Horse, the stone carving he had seen twenty years before. It was the one thing he really wanted to see, and he had talked about it enthusiastically at his good-bye party. We were about to make that wish come true.

Sean took his mother to breakfast, and I packed the bags and kept an eye on his father. He had slept pretty well. It was fairly easy to get him dressed and into the wheelchair. He was able to stand as we got his clothes arranged. The towel was working well. It was equally easy to get him settled in the front seat. Joan settled easily as well, and we were ready to go. I filled the travel mugs with really good coffee and jumped in the car. We left at 9:30 a.m. We had been up since seven. It took us that long to get ready.

Henry did not have a cigarette that morning. He woke up saying he had decided to quit. About an hour later, he spoke up.

"I think we should stop and check the oil. We haven't done that since we left home."

Sean and I looked at each other in the rearview mirror and smiled. We communicated very well with smiles, raised eyebrows, and gestures. This was one of the benefits of knowing each other so well—we didn't need to speak in order to communicate.

"Sure, Dad. There's a rest stop right ahead."

"Good. We need to check the oil, and the girls probably need to stretch their legs."

"A quick walk would be nice" I said, and Sean caught my eye again. We both knew we were stopping for a smoke break, and we both found the conversation amusing.

We pulled into the rest stop, and Joan and I took a trip to the ladies' room. I picked up some brochures on Crazy Horse, and Joan confused the ladies at the information desk by telling them, "Oh my.

Yep. It's what do you say, up, up, kind of like that, whatchamicallit, uh huh."

When we returned to the car, Sean had finished checking the oil and Henry was almost done with his cigarette.

"So how was the oil?"

"A few drops low. Good thing we checked. How was the ladies' room?" He smiled.

"Peachy."

"Nice. Well, let's get this show on the road."

"Are you doing okay, Sean?"

"I don't know." We hugged and climbed back in.

The smoke break was followed by lots of belching. I was glad we had converted an ice bucket from the inn into a travel-sized puke bucket. Apologies to the inn, but we didn't think they would want to keep it after it had been so well used the night before. Vomiting was now part of our trip experience.

ON THE ROAD TO CRAZY HORSE

The scenery was beautiful. Joan was really fascinated with those big round haystacks that looked like soup cans on their sides. She commented on them dozens of times, and as most sightings were "first sightings" for her, it was a real source of enjoyment.

She loved reading signs. As we drove through Rapid City, we passed signs for Red Ass Rhubarb Wine. She said it over and over with different inflections: RED ass rhubarb wine, red ASS rhubarb wine, RED ASS rhubarb wine. Between that and the Naked Winery, it was an entertaining morning as far as billboards went. The words sounded so funny coming out of her mouth.

I was the backseat navigator as we wound through the countryside in search of Crazy Horse. Just a few miles shy of the monument, we stopped in Hill City for gas. I loaded our coffee cups and bought a bag of popcorn for Henry. As I stood outside of his window, I asked him what he had in mind. Did he want to get out and tour the visitor's center? Did he want to be wheeled around the grounds? Did he want to pull onto the side of the road to look at it? What did he have in mind?

He told me he didn't want to get out of the car. He just wanted to see it and the changes that had happened over the past twenty years since his last visit. I was relieved to hear that, as he looked even worse than he had a few hours before when we got in the car. He was refusing liquids of any kind and hadn't eaten anything. I was able to get a few sips of fluid in him when I gave him his pills.

He was on more than a dozen medications, and getting them in him was becoming harder each day. I ended up choosing those that I felt were the most important and approaching him when he seemed most receptive. Interestingly, his pain levels had been dropping steadily as we traveled. I expected the opposite, but he was very clear about his comfort level and took pain medication only when he felt he needed it.

I was vigilant in telling him how long it had been since he had taken a pain pill and that I did not want him to "fall behind." It is much harder to play catch-up with escalating pain than it is to nip it in the bud. My goal was to maintain a level of pain meds that prevented severe episodes. For the most part, this strategy worked, and we never saw the truly terrible pain that cancer in the ribs and bones can cause.

He declined a pain pill and ate a few pieces of popcorn. He even tried a few tiny bites of a cereal bar. We loaded up and drove the final miles to our destination. Traffic was minimal, and we were soon at the entrance gate.

I had asked the clerk at the gas station if there was any type of scenic overlook that would allow us a good view of Crazy Horse. She saw the wheelchair in the back of our car and was very helpful. She told me that if we just wanted to take a picture, we should tell the gate staff; we would probably be allowed to drive just past the gate, take a peek, and turn around.

Sean told the man at the admission gate that we weren't going to stay, but we were hoping to take a photograph. He was very kind and directed us to the side of the road. He said we could take a look, snap a picture, and then turn around at the foot of the hill. Perfect…Sean pulled forward and angled the car to give his father a good view.

WHAT A DISAPPOINTMENT

"What a disappointment."

Those were the first words out of Henry's mouth. He stared at the mountainside and said, "It doesn't look any different. They haven't done anything in twenty years." He stopped looking.

Sean had gotten out of the car to take a photo of his father with Crazy Horse in the background. He took a photo for a passing biker, and our trip to Crazy Horse was over. The entire side trip lasted less than ten minutes.

What a disappointment.

Sean turned the car around, and we got back on the road. We decided to take Highway 16 into Wyoming, a path none of us had taken before. It looked to be closer than backtracking through Rapid City. Within a few minutes, we approached Custer, and the signs were not very clear. As Sean pulled into a parking lot to turn around, Henry vomited.

Sean tended to his father while I went into a store to ask for directions. The clerk sent us in the opposite direction, but we figured it out in less than a block and corrected our course. Onward to Wyoming, the fourth state in our journey.

It was a beautiful day, and there was much to look at. Henry missed most of it because his eyes were closed. As we closed in on Wyoming, the scenery went through rapid changes. There were areas where the trees were dead and the earth scorched. Whether by wildfires or by design, it was not pretty. Upon seeing one of these patches, Joan said, "Someone started it, those dirty rats."

She came up with some pretty funny lines. At about this time, I started making notes. I had joked about writing a book before we ever left Wisconsin, but by our third day I knew I wanted to really write one.

Henry was very quiet. He wasn't holding himself upright very well, and the belching and groaning was getting more frequent.

"It's been almost three hours since you had your pain medication, Henry. Would you like one now?" I asked.

"Nope. Don't need it."

"Can I get you anything to drink? We have lots of choices, and I would really like to see you drink a little."

"No, I'm not thirsty."

"Can I interest you in a few of your pills? You haven't taken any of them yet today, and I think your heart meds would be a good start."

"Yeah, okay. You're the boss."

I handed him his pills and he chased them with a sip of flavored water.

We listened to classical music. It was a good compromise. We all liked classical. While Sean's parents could happily listen to the same four CDs over and over again, they just didn't bring the same level of enjoyment to Sean and me. We had heard them many, many times. We had been pretty lucky about finding good stations, though, and driving through Jewel Cave National Monument while listening to classical music is not a bad way to spend an afternoon.

About ninety minutes after leaving Crazy Horse, Henry opened his eyes and said, "I don't know about you, but I am tired of sitting on my arse." He had a little coughing fit.

Joan spoke up, "Stop doing that—you sound like you are dying."

"Sorry."

Joan went back to looking at the scorched scenery. She had no idea he really was dying.

GILLETTE, WYOMING

Henry was not doing well and needed to stop. The nearest town with services was Gillette. As we drove toward it, I calculated how many hours left until we got home and how we could make it there as quickly as possible.

I wanted to get into Montana. I was trying to figure out how to get Henry to Washington alive. I recognized the sinking, and it scared me a little. I didn't want Sean to have to make a life-and-death decision in a hotel room. I didn't want him to feel as if he had failed his father.

The first hotel we tried didn't have handicapped or adjoining rooms. Sean and I had gone inside to ask about availability. We were both anxious to get out of the car for a few minutes, and while Sean was looking for a bathroom and I was standing at the front desk, Joan hopped out of the car, wandered in the door, and headed into the lounge. I just happened to turn around and see her as she walked by. She could have easily escaped my attention.

Lesson learned. If we ever got out of the car together again, we would remember to use the child locks to prevent an escape from the backseat. There was nothing Henry could do to stop her or alert us. He didn't have the energy. That could have been a very serious mistake. Joan was very trusting and might have gone with anyone who held out a hand.

In looking for a hotel room, we needed an open door between us. We were lucky to get two beautiful rooms at the Fairfield Inn next door. Sean and I checked the layout before booking the room and practically lifted Henry into the wheelchair to get him out of the car and into bed. He was asleep at 3 p.m. He had eaten next to nothing and refused all drinks I had offered.

His mood was declining as his energy evaporated. Joan was restless. Sean and I took turns leaving the hotel so we could do a little shopping and get some air. We were both exhausted. He took a walk to Walmart, and then I went to Walgreens. I searched for what I thought I would need: Pedialyte drink mix, a dropper that delivered one teaspoon of fluid at a time, and a thermometer that read skin temperature and would not disturb him.

I got back to the hotel and started doing laundry. Both Joan and Henry had soiled their clothing, and laundry was piling up. Two loads in three days. It gave me something to do. Sean read and watched his father. I took his mom for a few walks, and we found the hot chocolate chip cookies at the desk. She liked them and ate three. I had two. We admired the vases and fake plants as we walked around.

That evening was the first time cracks developed between Sean and me. We were talking about the next day, and Sean said, "There are five days until you have to be back. If he needs to rest, we can stay here." We were not looking at the situation the same way. Sean thought short days would not be as taxing on his father. I looked at the situation like a clock winding down.

There was a definite tension between us, and I could feel Sean's anger rolling off him in waves and heading my direction. I was not about to let it simmer.

"Sean, I need to know what you're thinking and am worried we are running out of time."

"If he needs to rest for a day or two, we can stay here. You don't have to be back for five days."

"I don't think we have five days. If we stay here an extra day we may never leave."

"We may have to take that chance. If he isn't up to it, we can't go."

"Sean, I thought the whole point of this was that your dad wanted to see your mom settled into her new home. That is the whole reason for making this trip, isn't it? To get to Washington? If we are going to get there, you may have to start making the decisions."

"It's up to Dad. We'll see how he feels in the morning."

"I want you to understand that we have to work together, and I need you to talk to me. I don't think your father has five days left.

Do you want him to spend his final days in a hotel room in Wyoming or trying to get to Washington? I need you to hear that if we stay, I think he will only get weaker and we may not make it."

"Let's try to get a good night's sleep and we'll make a decision in the morning. Maybe he just needs a good night's rest. He's been sleeping since we got here."

I recognized that Sean would be the one to make the call about what we did. It was his father. I was frustrated. He was frustrated. This was not at all the trip we had agreed on and prepared for. Sean's response to fatigue and stress was to lash out, and I happened to be the one sitting next to him. I simply did not have the energy for his anger and frustration, so I did what I do when I am stressed: keep busy.

It was a trait that drove him crazy at times, but it also came in very handy. I did laundry, and he read. We got through the evening as best we could, picking up a pizza to keep things simple for the two of us and his mother. We tried not to get in each other's way. We needed to be on the same page, but that evening was not an example of teamwork.

I found some comfort in checking my emails and writing to my friend Louise. She was dealing with her own mother's recent health crisis, and we were keeping tabs on each other. My email that evening was straight to the point: "We are in a hotel in Gillette, Wyoming, and I don't know if Sean's dad will live through the night. He has a DNR so we are just letting him rest and providing drops of fluid, pain meds, and support. Long story, foolish plan but he had his last wish—to see Crazy Horse, of all things. I'll call you whenever I get home. Hope your mom is getting better."

His father had been sleeping since we checked in, and the three of us were tucked in at about 9:00 p.m. Sean got a decent night's sleep. I did not. His mom was up at 11 p.m., both parents were awake and needing attention at midnight, his mom was up again at 2:00 a.m. and they both were up at 4 a.m.

Sean managed to sleep through his mother's forays into our room. I was up every time his parents awoke. I woke Sean to help his father. I finally gave up on sleep at around 5 a.m., when I went outside to rearrange the car in case we needed to turn Henry's seat into a bed.

That was something else we had not agreed on the night before. I had come up with a plan to allow Henry's chair to recline fully if he needed to be in that position. This would have required using one of the third row seats. Sean had not agreed with my thinking, and he was right. My plan would not have worked. I was needed behind his father, and his mom would not willingly have climbed into the third row. At least the car was clean and as organized as possible when we loaded up Wednesday morning.

WEDNESDAY, JULY 27

Everyone was up at around 7 a.m. I took advantage of the lovely bathroom to get Joan into the shower. We washed her hair and got her all cleaned up. I took Joan down to breakfast and tanked up on coffee. Joan was in a quiet mood.

Sean and his father had a chat while we were gone. When Joan and I got back to the room, Sean was sitting quietly at his father's bedside. Sean looked resigned, and Henry looked disheveled and worn out. The room felt overwhelmingly sad. Sean went down for breakfast, and Joan sat at the foot of her bed watching *Good Morning America*.

Henry was restless. He had wet the bed and needed dry clothes. I asked him if I could give him a bed bath. He said yes, and I started cleaning him up. It started a little awkwardly, but we got past that quickly. I made the necessary jump from their family friend to nurse. We both accepted that change. Family friend…I'll come back to that later.

When I got up to his arms, he grabbed me and very clearly said, "I'm not going to make it, am I?"

"To Washington?"

"Yes. I'm not going to make it, am I?"

I looked him in the eye and answered with a question of my own:

"Do you remember telling me you wanted this trip to be more of a vacation and less of an ambulance ride but wanted to get to Washington conscious? Do you remember that conversation?"

Henry looked right into my eyes and said, "I remember."

"Well, I think we can get you to Washington, but the vacation is over. This needs to be an ambulance ride. I think we can get you into the car one more time, but once we are in, we need to make a run for it. Do you understand?"

"I understand. You think we can make it?"

"Sean and I will drive all day and all night to get you to Washington, but I honestly don't know if you will be conscious or not. Is that what you want us to do? Do you want to make a run for it?"

"Yes."

It was a quiet and logical conversation. I promised we would get him to Washington and make sure Joan was safe and protected.

When Sean returned, we went into our room for a quick chat. I was trying not to cry, but tears were spilling.

"I asked him if he remembered telling me he didn't want it be an ambulance ride, and he did. I told him I thought we could get him there and were willing to try."

"What did he say?"

"He told me he wanted to get to Washington, Sean. I think if we get in that car, we will need to drive until we get there. I don't think he has another trip in and out of the car left in him. I think this is it."

"It's going to be a long day."

"I know. We'll do the best we can."

I cried a little, and we hugged. We both knew there was no guarantee we would make it. Sean talked with his father again, and we got ready.

In preparing for a bad outcome, I had pulled out the copy of his do not resuscitate order and the armband that went with it. I was glad we at least had that order specifying what he did and did not want done.

I would have felt so much better about our chances if I could have started an IV and given him a few liters of fluid, but that wasn't an option. We continued to give him fluid a dropper at a time. He seemed to like the Pedialyte I had purchased the day before, and it was packed in the car right next to the puke bucket. My half of the backseat was getting more crowded.

It was harder getting him in the car this morning. Sean supported most of his father's body weight as he slid Henry into the seat. I believed we wouldn't be able to do that again. It was the combined determination of Sean and his father that got him in the car that morning.

WHERE IS MY WALLET?

Once Henry was settled into the car, Sean went back into the hotel to do a last walk-through of the rooms. I helped Joan get her seat belt on. Sometimes she was able to put it on herself without difficulty, but this was not one of those mornings. As I stretched the belt across her upper body, she grabbed it and put it behind her head, where it got tangled in the prayer shawl. I tried many times while standing next to her at her door and finally had to go around the car, climb into the backseat, and reach across her, putting my body between her chest and the belt. Once it was on, she was fine. It just took a while.

While Joan and I worked on her seat belt, Henry tried to open the compartment between the front seats. There were two compartments: a shallow upper tray and a deep space underneath. The latches could be a little difficult to open. He got very upset and began saying, "Where's my wallet?" over and over again as he struggled to open the compartments. He was so frantic that it scared me. He was shaking the compartment, and his voice got increasingly loud and agitated.

I ran around the car and stood outside his door. I tried to calm him but was not successful. I reached over to try to open the compartment while telling him Sean would be right out and would open the compartment and show him his wallet. I was unable to open the latch because Henry would not let go of it. I told him we were okay and that we would not leave without his wallet. He could not hear what I was saying as he was in a full-blown panic. He was shaking and flailing his arms and yelling, "Where's my wallet? Where's my wallet? I need my wallet!"

Sean arrived as I tried in vain to calm Henry. I stepped aside, and Sean stood next to his father, putting his hand in the middle of his father's chest. He said, "Hold on, Dad. I'll get it for you." He was able to move Henry's hand out of the way and open the compartment. The wallet was right there. He handed it to Henry, who held it tightly. Sean walked around the car, and we both buckled up. As he started the engine, he asked his father if they should put the wallet away. Henry handed it to him, closed his eyes, and went to sleep.

THE BIG PUSH

We left Gillette at 8:38 a.m. Three days of driving had gotten us 964 miles. We weren't even halfway home yet and were running out of time. Both Sean and I were quiet as we tried to come to grip with the rapid changes.

For Sean, it was the loss of the life he had envisioned for his parents once they got there. They had a beautiful apartment, and he had wanted to show them the area he loved so much. We had discussed many times that it would be a wonderful place to spend your final months.

The facility they were moving into had huge windows that looked out over the town, the bay, and the Olympic Mountains. It was a truly spectacular view. We had hoped they would be very happy there. The plan had been for them to share the apartment for as long as possible until Joan needed to move into the memory care unit. Henry would be able to see his wife settled and well cared-for before he died. That was the plan.

Now we needed a new plan. There was no possibility Henry could participate in any supervision or care of his wife, and there was no opening in memory care. Months of discussions, planning, and preparations had to be abandoned as it became clear that Sean now had two parents who would need constant care and/or supervision. We needed a Plan B, and we needed one quickly.

As we crossed into Montana, I saw mile marker 551. That's a lot of miles to cover, and we still had Idaho and a large part of Washington after that. Henry would occasionally ask how many miles we had driven. Starting with the first day, he would calculate how far we had come. The first night, for example, we came about 10 percent of the way.

It was a question he would ask throughout the day: how many miles had we driven and were we in Washington yet? As we started to cross Montana, it felt like we would never get there.

HOW LOW CAN YOU GO?

Our first stop of the day was in Billings. It was time to get gas, use the bathroom, and change drivers. This pit stop was one of the lowest moments of the trip—at least for me.

I chose the exit so will take the blame. It was a commercial strip, but there were few gas stations and no easy access. Sean went down the road, turned off into a parking lot, circled around, and then headed back toward the first gas station we had passed. His phone was ringing, and I really had to pee.

When we finally pulled into the gas station, we saw it was undergoing a renovation and the bathrooms were two side-by-side Honey Buckets in the parking lot. I have an aversion to these port-a-potties, but I needed to use the bathroom and so did Joan. One was handicapped accessible, and we went in together.

Joan went first, and as she sat down, she promptly put her hand in the urinal to pick up a piece of tissue. I wasn't fast enough to stop her and my, "No Joan. NO!" was lost on her. How disgusting is a port-a-potty urinal? I had to try to clean that hand with the antibacterial lotion on the wall as she tried to pee while hovering above the opening. This was not one of our finest moments.

I washed her hands three or four times, then opened the door and went looking for Sean. I needed a moment alone—even if it was in a parking lot Honey Bucket. When I was done and returned to the car, it was to find Henry sleeping in the front seat with a lit cigarette burning down toward his fingers. Sean saw it at the same time and woke his father before he was burned.

I got behind the wheel, and we pulled away from the pumps so Henry could finish his cigarette. That image is one that will stay with me forever. A very ill man who was marginally coherent but still trying to smoke. I believe that was his last cigarette. It was so very sad.

ON THE ROAD AGAIN

We pulled back on the highway, and I started speeding. I was slowed at times by construction, but I wasn't wasting any time. Somewhere east of Bozeman, Henry reached over and took my hand.

He started talking in fragments, and it was clear he was elsewhere. He talked about paying $18 for removing a patch, keeping battery acid away from the kids, and asking where his wife's sister and brother-in-law were. He seemed to be in varying times and places. I answered as best I could, but I do not know if he heard me.

He took my hand several times and then started grabbing at the gearshift. The car was automatic, but it made me nervous. I put my hand under his on the shift, and we kept going. He pointed out the window once and said, "We could have dinner there. See, I'm pointing it out." He wanted to stop "for a bite."

During this part of our drive, he started picking at the air. I knew this was common in people who were approaching death. It can be from decreased oxygen to the brain, anxiety, or pain. It can be for many reasons. It let me know this was as serious as we thought it was.

Earlier in the day, he had reached over, turned off the radio, and turned on his CDs. He later turned the CDs off as well. I turned his favorite music back on at a low volume and held his hand when he allowed me to.

I told him we were on the way to Washington. I told him he was doing great and we would get to Washington as fast as we could. I looked over many times to see if he was breathing. Sean started making calls from the backseat to let the ALF in Washington know we were making a run for it.

Joan was blessedly unaware of the growing sense of urgency. She continued to look through her photo album, admire Ronald Reagan, and look out the window. She enjoyed the big bales of hay and varied shades of green. While I thought the rocky formations were beautiful, she stated often that they were messy and "too much there." Tall trees seemed to distress her; she would say things like "just too much" or that it was "way out there."

She was dismayed by her husband's messy hair, and it had certainly seen better days. She pointed it out to me many times that day, telling me, "Daddy should fix his hair." I tried to comb it out a few times, but it never met with her approval. Hair care is definitely not in my skill set.

At 3:30 p.m., we crossed the continental divide. Progress. As we approached Butte, Sean suggested we pull over and take a break. We stopped at a very nice little gas station, and Joan and I had a far better bathroom experience. We got cold drinks, coffee, and chocolate.

There would be no lunch this day. There would be no break for dinner. We ate out of the food box. No one went hungry, and neither Sean nor I would have considered stopping for a meal.

Sean got in the driver's seat, and I went back to my place behind Henry. I had learned several days before that I had a great view of his face through the side view mirror, and that is how I watched him. He was having a harder time sitting up, and we tried varying degrees of reclining in his seat. I am only five feet tall, so he could come way back if needed. He was not comfortable in any position, though, and we did a lot of rearranging.

The Power of Texting

I am one of those people who did not want to become a texter. I have a very basic phone, and it works fine for me. I purposely tried to avoid texting, and as I had been rear-ended by someone who was texting, I thought it was a good policy. If I wanted to talk with someone, I would call. Antiquated idea, I know, but I just didn't want to add "LOL," "TTYL," and "LMAO" to my vocabulary.

The first summer I worked at camp in Washington, this had been a source of amusement and amazement to members of the staff. The program director was named James, a soon-to-be college senior who was completely baffled by this concept. He heard my reasons and said, "Well, my parents took a long time to come around, too." Ouch.

Times change, though, and in the first half of 2011, I had become a texter out of necessity. It was the best way to stay in touch with Sean when he was in Wisconsin. There was poor cell reception at his parent's house, but for some reason texts would go through. When we talked on his parent's landline, I could hear every word of CNN, *Matlock*, or the *Golden Girls*. Sean and I could communicate with very few words, though, so texting became our link when we were apart.

My sister also helped pull me into the age of texting. She has two little boys at home who do not believe in letting her talk on the phone without adding impressive levels of background noise. My youngest nephew has a very healthy set of lungs and displayed his yelling capacity almost very time I called. I did not want to be the one to wake up a sleeping child, so we started texting. It allowed us to say hello quietly.

The first day of camp I was talking with James when I got a text. It was from a friend in Texas and made me smile. I sent a quick reply and heard James say, "OMG, you joined the herd. You text now? I never expected you to do that." He found it funny that I had changed policies, especially since I had explained it was a matter of principle the year before. I rather sheepishly admitted that I had accepted that texts were here to stay and I understood their value. He started texting me that day.

Camp was in session when I left for Wisconsin, and I had kept in touch with both James and the recreation director. They gave me updates on how campers I knew were doing and how my counselors were doing. Although my time with these young people was brief, I truly cared about their experience as counselors and hoped that some of them would join the field. I tried very hard to show them that communication, teamwork, and looking at the common goal and common good was very important both at camp and once they left. I hope my message got through.

As we were driving, I would get occasional texts from my two camp friends. They wanted me to know they were thinking of me. They gave me tidbits from camp and asked how we were doing. I was also getting texts from my sister and my friend Louise. My phone didn't always work, but when we were in range of a cell tower, it would chirp to let me know I had messages waiting. It truly is the little things in life that are so special—the message chirp let me know I was not alone and gave me much-needed contact with life beyond the backseat.

While I was thrilled to hear my phone signal the arrival of a new text, Henry was not so happy about it. I had turned off the volume after it woke him the first time, but even the vibration of the phone was enough to wake him or cause him to "humph" and squirm when it went off. I was not willing to turn the phone off, so I wrapped it in a washcloth and tried to minimize the beautiful buzz that told me someone "out there" cared.

CELL PHONES AND SIGNALS
IN WESTERN MONTANA

I tried reaching hospice in our county to see if they could arrange delivery of a hospital bed and oxygen. Cell phone reception is spotty in western Montana, and several calls were dropped or missed. It became a game of calling whenever a signal popped up and leaving messages.

I also called the director of the ALF to let him know what was happening and to confirm that their apartment would be ready. He was understandably alarmed by the change in Henry's condition and at one point left us a message suggesting we drive directly to the hospice facility.

I called hospice to see if that was even a possibility, which started a wave of calls between two hospice nurses, the operator, and me. On hearing of his deterioration, it was suggested that we stop at the Spokane hospice for an assessment. There were no beds available in our county.

The nurses were very nice and knowledgeable. I listened to their thoughts and said I would discuss the options with Henry's son and call back when we had a signal. They knew we were approaching Idaho and were concerned the trip was too ambitious. They said it was our decision, but we had to face the fact that he might die in the car.

Sean was driving and looking at his father's chest whenever he could. We were thinking the same thing as the hospice nurses: he might die before we got there. He was hallucinating, belching, and groaning at intervals. He answered no to pain when I asked, but I gave him morphine at our last stop. As he got more restless, I gave him Ativan as well, and that seemed to help a little.

He hadn't urinated since we left the hotel, and this was concerning. His fluid intake had been minimal, but it was a definite change. It was concerning to the hospice nurse I talked with as well.

I relayed the conversations to Sean as we drove. I offered to have a discussion outside of the car, but he declined and kept driving. I told him about the Spokane possibility and said he would have to make the call.

Out of nowhere, Sean said, "Well, I have to think about maintaining his dignity."

I have no idea where that comment came from, but it seemed to be aimed at me. It felt like a slap in the face, like Sean was suggesting that I was ignoring his father's needs, and I reacted strongly.

Sean said I should not take it personally. A few minutes later, he reached out and put his hand on my knee. I had a short, silent cry in the backseat. I was exhausted and Sean was as well. We didn't need to be in conflict.

Joan didn't notice anything was wrong and didn't seem to listen to the phone calls. She was preoccupied with the back cover of the "Ronald Reagan at 100" issue. It was an advertisement for an issue covering one hundred people who changed the world and had photos of various people.

She made comments about the pictures she recognized and even some she didn't. She knew Jesus and said he was a good boy. Hitler, on the other hand, had an ugly mustache and was a bad boy. Lincoln looked sad but was good. She did not recognize Oprah but was of the opinion that her hair was quite "floofy." Einstein also fared badly in the hair department. She just grimaced and said, "Tut, tut, tut."

Mother Teresa perplexed her. She thought she was probably a very nice lady but looked very tired and possibly ill. The Beatles escaped her attention entirely. Nelson Mandela looked to be celebrating his birthday, and Gandhi looked hungry.

It was very disjointed to discuss Hitler, Jesus, and Oprah's hair between calls to hospice. I was talking about good boy Jesus, offering snacks from the food box, watching Henry breath through the rear view mirror, confirming that an apartment was ready, retrieving messages on both mine and Sean's phones, and trying to support my friend as he had to make some choices for his father.

East of the Idaho line, Henry started saying he needed the urinal so we pulled over. I got out to help him and applied pressure on his bladder. It was flat. He urinated a very small amount. The hospice nurse had said the picking could be from a full bladder, but that was not the case. He started urinating very small amounts at increasingly short intervals, which led to multiple stops.

One of these stops was right off the highway in Idaho. I don't remember where, but as we exited, there was a chained fence to some sort of utility facility right off the road. It was good as any place else, so we pulled over. I helped Henry urinate, and I am pretty sure Sean took advantage of the shrubbery to grab a quick pee. I needed to go as well and there were no facilities in sight.

I made the executive decision that I could justify peeing right there on the roadside. As I prepared to do exactly that, Joan hopped out of her side of the car directly into the road. We had forgotten the child lock, and she decided it was a good time to stretch her legs. Traffic appeared out of nowhere, and my window of opportunity was gone.

Sean stopped once more shortly after this, and we were hopeful it would be the last stop for a while. I took Joan to the bathroom, bought some drinks and food, and went back out to help Henry try to urinate again. We were getting an increasing sense of anger from him as he would say not very nicely, "Help me, help me." He did not recognize that we could not always pull over the second he told us he needed to pee. When we went through an area of constructions with cones and barriers, he got quite angry with us, swearing and telling us to help him.

We were using all of the Crazy Frank's pillows, multiple towels, and the prayer blanket to find a comfortable position for Henry. I had brought my Total Pillow (as seen on TV) with me, and it worked beautifully as a headrest. He was having difficulty staying upright, however, and by the time we hit the Washington State line, I was sitting forward and supporting the left side of the Total Pillow as I held his head in place.

WASHINGTON

We saw the signs for Spokane, and I looked at Sean. He motioned that we were going to keep driving.

"Henry," I said. "We made it to Washington."

He said, "West, west, west."

"You're doing great. We made it to Washington, and we will get you home."

He didn't answer.

I made one last call to hospice and told the nurse of our decision. She wished us luck and asked us to call at 8:01 a.m. so the admitting nurse could talk with us and arrange to be at the ALF when we arrived. 8:01 seemed like a long ways away.

The drive across Washington seemed to take forever. We had to pull over many times when Henry said he needed to urinate. We got lost in downtown Spokane and stopped on the side of the road several times. The temperature had dropped, and Joan was cold when we took our final bathroom break. We held hands and hustled into the bathroom. She had the prayer shawl wrapped around her, and when I turned to get toilet paper for her, the corner went in the toilet. She stuck her whole hand in the toilet to retrieve it, and I ended up doing the wiping. A quick wash at the sink and we were back in the car.

Sean and I spoke very little. There was nothing to say. I touched his shoulder and ask if he was doing okay. I watched the mile markers decrease ever so slowly. I wanted to cry. I'm sure Sean did as well. We were in survival mode. He kept driving, and I kept holding Henry's head as he dozed. Joan fell asleep somewhere in the middle of the state. She was clutching a Sprite and a pad of paper on which she had written, "I love frogs." She would later be puzzled as to who wrote that since she didn't even like frogs.

As we finally approached Seattle, it was past midnight and we didn't have a ferry schedule. Driving around the water made more sense, so we just kept going. When we passed SeaTac airport, we knew we were an hour away.

"What is the plan for when we get there?" I asked.

"I have no idea," Sean said. "Maybe a hotel. I don't think we could get him into my house. What are you thinking?"

"My suggestion would be to go to my house. There is a ramp outside, and it is a straight shot to my bed. I think the chair would fit through the door. He would be comfortable there, and there's plenty of room for us. I have the inflatable beds, and the couch would be fine."

"We could grab sleeping bags from my place on the way. That's okay with you, bringing the show to your house?"

"I know he has never seen my house, but I think it would feel more welcoming and comfortable than another hotel, and we don't know if there will be any handicapped rooms. It makes sense to me, and in the morning we can figure out how to get him to the ALF."

"Sounds like a plan, Stan."

"Okey dokey, artichokey."

The ALF wouldn't let us move in until 9 a.m. the next morning. I didn't know exactly how we were going to get him out of the car, but I thought that if tonight were to be his final night, it would be better for him to be in a home. We had been in the car for almost nineteen hours when we finally got there. Sean had done almost all of the driving that day, keeping a constant watch on the rise and fall of his father's chest.

We stopped at Sean's house so I could grab keys and sleeping bags, and we went to my house. I ran inside to clear a path to the bed while Sean got the wheelchair ready. It was a little after 3:00 a.m. Joan had started walking down the street, and once I caught her, I turned her around, took her hand, and led her inside.

She walked around my house, admiring the art on the walls. She looked at each piece carefully and told me she liked them. She did not notice the stress and struggle going on around her. I am glad for that.

Getting Henry out of the car was traumatic for all three of us. He could not help at all and was crying out, "No! You are going to drop me!" Sean and I assured him we would keep him safe. He struggled against us as we tried to get him out of the car. We finally just slid him out as best we could into the wheelchair and backed into the house, with Sean pulling the chair and me carrying his legs. We lifted him onto my bed and unloaded what we needed like zombies.

Joan slept on my couch wrapped in a comforter and went to sleep very quickly. We got Henry settled and put down a sleeping bag and an air mattress on my office floor so we could try to sleep for a few hours. Within five minutes, Henry was calling for Sean. He was agitated and thought he needed to urinate. This would be repeated many times over the next hour or so. I heard the frustration and pleading in Sean's voice when he asked his father to please try to sleep. "Twenty hours, Dad. I need some rest. Please try to just relax."

Sean was desperate for sleep. I moved my mattress out of the office, shut the door, and gave him the gift of uninterrupted sleep. I got Henry settled a little after 4:00 a.m., and at 4:45 a.m., Joan was up and rearranging my living room. I tried to get her back to sleep, and it lasted maybe twenty minutes. I think I got about sixty minutes of sleep that night.

At 6:30 a.m., Joan was on her second breakfast and I was on my third cup of coffee. Henry called that he wanted to get out of bed and stand up. I knew that was not possible. I woke Sean up because I needed help. This was no longer a job for one person. It took both of us. Sean caught up on coffee, and we got ready for another long day.

MAKING ARRANGEMENTS

Our strategy was to divide and conquer. Sean tended to his father and kept his mother occupied while I called hospice to ask about the possibility of getting an ambulance transfer to the ALF. This was not a possibility as he was not yet an official hospice patient. The hospice nurse said he would meet us at the ALF as soon as we arrived to do the admission. In the meantime, we needed to arrange for transportation.

I called the ALF to verify that the hospital bed and oxygen system had been delivered. They had, and I was told the staff was "sprucing up" the apartment to make it feel more welcoming. All we had was what we had put in the car and what I had purchased before leaving for Wisconsin. The minimal furnishings packed into the cube had not yet arrived. The apartment was ready, though, and that was great news.

I made copies of Henry's insurance cards and license: one set for me and one set for Sean. I called an ambulance service to arrange for transport. They asked why we needed an ambulance. I told the dispatcher that we could not get him back in the car and did not think he could sit up. We scheduled an 11:00 a.m. pickup for the one-mile trip to the ALF.

There was little to eat in my house. I certainly had not planned for this. I had already given Joan the only yogurt I had and the last of the cereal bars. I did a quick hunt and came up with frozen pizza. Sean and I are both fans of pizza. We used to make our own from scratch during football season. This wasn't going to be on par with some of our former creations, but it sounded pretty good. When it was done, Sean and I both grabbed slices between calls, position changes, urinal duty, and bath time. It tasted great.

"More coffee?" I asked after we drained the first pot.

"There can't be enough coffee," Sean responded, and I agreed. We both loved coffee, and when we lived together we were a two-pot-per-day household. We took turns refilling each other's cups. It was one of our little rituals.

While we were waiting for the ambulance, I decided to make a bubble bath for Joan. My mom kept me exceptionally well stocked in Bath & Body Works products, and I thought Joan might enjoy a bath. She had been up for hours, walking around the house. She had been looking at things, moving things around, and reading anything in her path. She was not interested in sitting still.

At one point, she was in my home office and picked up my business card from one of those little acrylic card-holders. She looked at, smiled, and said my name out loud exclaiming, "I know her!" I asked Joan how she knew her (me) and she did not answer, opting for the "He he he" breathing that meant there wasn't an answer coming. Joan had two responses that let us know she was out of her comfort zone. She would say, "Yup, yup, yup," or do a breathing pattern of, "He, he, he." It was sort of like Lamaze, but much quieter. Either answer told us to change the subject.

Joan had a nice bath. She spent a long time drying herself as she kept starting over. She was meticulous about drying between her toes but almost always chose to do this by putting her foot on the toilet seat. This, of course, led to dipping the towel in the toilet. That led to needing another towel and staring the process over again. We managed to get her clean, dry, and dressed. She was very good at brushing her teeth, but she could not find a hairstyle she liked, telling me she "looked like crap."

The foyer of my apartment was a mess. We had dropped our bags there the night before, and all of those suitcases were too much of a temptation for Joan. She quickly added a second outfit over the first. As it was her husband's, it fit easily over her sweater. She was rummaging for a third layer when I asked her to help me pack so we could continue with our trip. I was able to remove the second layer so she could arrive at the ALF in one well-matched outfit.

MOVING DAY

The ambulance arrived on time, and the staff was very nice as they gathered information and got ready to transfer Henry onto a stretcher. I was in full nurse mode and gave the EMS crew the same report I would give in an ICU. One of them looked at me and said, "Nurse?"

"It shows? Sorry, I am really tired and probably gave you way too much information."

"Just the opposite. I have no questions, and we are good to go."

Sean asked me to take Joan in my car, thinking that the ambulance and stretcher might be distressing to her. We walked right by the ambulance staff, and she didn't bat an eye. She was concerned with the dirt on my black car, though. It had been sitting under a tree for the past week and was covered with dust, small droplets of sap, and assorted offerings from passing birds. I told her we would go to the drive-through car wash and she got right in.

We stopped at the post office, and I grabbed my mail. She really liked the huge hanging flower baskets that lined the streets of our little town. We drove through a car wash and then headed to the ALF. We arrived ahead of the ambulance and walked in. I introduced Joan to the lady at the reception desk, and she called for the administrator, who I will call Robert.

He joined us quickly with a welcome and friendly smile. We had met once before, and I introduced him to Joan. Joan was very friendly and patted him on the arm. He welcomed her and asked if he could show us to her new home. Her answer was, "Well, I guess so. You gotta, well, someone, whatever it takes." When we got on the elevator, he asked her where she got her beautiful necklace, and she answered, "Yup, yup, yup."

He smiled and patted her shoulder. It was nice to be around people who knew to drop a topic when it was clear it wasn't in her repertoire. We walked down the hall and entered the apartment,

#319. They had done a great job. It was completely furnished with a love seat, TV, dining room set, and bed with a dresser and nightstands. They would later bring a recliner, a few lamps, and a CD player with tapes they thought would be enjoyed. I was, and still am, touched by the efforts made to welcome us.

Joan and I were touring the apartment when the ambulance arrived. We saw it out of the living room window. She watched them unload her husband, but she showed no sign of recognition. She said, "Someone must be sick."

Our afternoon was really hectic. Henry needed to be admitted by hospice, there was paperwork to be completed for both of Sean's parents for the ALF, the ALF nursing staff needed to do assessments, and various staff members came by to both welcome us and introduce themselves. Sean took a few minutes to go down to the dining room to have lunch with his mom. I stayed with his father.

"You'll be okay with Dad? I'll be as fast as I can, but there's no telling how Mom will do."

"Take your time. We'll be fine. I'll call you if anyone shows up before you're done."

"You can take the lead with the hospice nurse if that's okay. You know everything as well as I do, probably better. If you don't mind, that is. I know you speak the language."

"That's fine. I can handle the medical and you can handle all of the paperwork. You'll have to sign everything, but I can certainly fill them in on anything medical."

"Thanks, Beanie." Sean looked completely exhausted. I thought he might be worried I was going to leave once his parents were settled in, and I knew he would have a hard time asking me how long I was going to stay.

"I'm not going anywhere, Sean. I won't leave you to deal with this alone. We aren't close to being done. You're not alone here, okay?"

He shook his head. We hugged and he whispered, "I love you. Thank you. Thank you."

I wasn't staying just for Sean. I was staying for Joan and Henry, who had been my second parents for more than twenty-five years. They had been very generous to me when I was a poor college student, and when I graduated from nursing school they sat next to my mom and dad. The four of us went back to 1981, and I was not going to leave Sean alone to face what I knew was coming.

The hospice nurse arrived while Sean and his mom were at lunch. I gave him the background information, and while we were going over medications, Sean came back.

Henry was answering questions clearly. He told the nurse he was not in pain. He was cooperative, and the nurse did a very thorough exam. During this exam, Robert knocked on the door with a questionnaire to be completed for each parent. Sean sat down to fill out the questionnaires, and I stayed with his father and the hospice nurse. If Sean needed input, I walked out to help answer questions for the ALF, and when the hospice nurse asked me something I didn't know, I would get Sean. It was stressful to do both at once, but it needed to be done. Sean's mom was watching TV, reading magazines, and trying to straighten Henry's covers.

The nurse was concerned that Henry hadn't had a bowel movement since we left Wisconsin. Although his food intake was minimal, it is still important to address constipation. The nurse said we could give him an enema or we could manually check for an impaction (stool in the rectum). He asked if that was something I had done or would be able to do.

I was silent for a second. He looked at me and very quietly said, "That's something that might be too uncomfortable for you. Some lines shouldn't be crossed, right?" I agreed. I had become Henry's nurse, but I just did not feel comfortable doing a manual check of his bowels. I said I was happy to assist him, but that I would prefer if he did it.

The nurse got permission from Henry and performed a manual dis-impaction. Henry was answering the nurse, who was doing an admiral job of trying to distract him from an uncomfortable and invasive procedure. As the nurse said he was almost done, Henry said,

"Fine with me. You're the boss." I said, "Hold on there. I thought I was the boss." Henry said that yes, absolutely, I was still the boss. He even laughed a little. That was a welcome sound.

There was quite a bit of stool that needed to come out, so after removing what he could, we agreed on a suppository. This was the point where we went to a diaper. The ALF staff had found a package of diapers for us, and we put one on Henry while waiting for the suppository to do its work. Henry was tired from the exam and procedures and fell asleep quickly. The nurse and I finished up with the paperwork, and Sean signed where he needed to.

Before he left, the hospice nurse confirmed there would be a case conference the following afternoon. He also gave me a few suggestions as to what cremation services we could contact. I had asked him about that as I thought a hospice nurse would be the best possible resource concerning end-of-life issues. In two minutes, he saved us a significant amount of time and stress.

We were alone again: Sean, Henry, Joan, and I. Sean unloaded the car, and I unpacked their bags. I took a brief break to run back to my house to get what I would need to stay. It had become very clear to us both that, although we had made it to the ALF, we were far from done. I picked up my inflatable mattress and packed a bag. I wasn't going to leave Sean alone.

CHECKING INTO THE ALF

Later that afternoon, Robert returned with the mountain of paperwork that is required when moving into an ALF. Henry was pretty comfortable and sleeping. Joan was in a good mood. Sean and I sat down with Robert to go over the paperwork. When he learned that we would be staying, he quickly offered to have a bed brought up for Sean. Sean had been planning on getting a cot from Walmart, but this was a better and more comfortable solution.

Robert let us know there might be an opening in memory care for Joan. There was an open bed, but it was being held while a family discussed moving their mother from the ALF side into memory care. He would know for sure the following day.

This facility was set up like many others. Most of the residents lived on the assisted living side, with private apartments and common areas like the dining room, game room, lobby, and multiple little coffee shop–type rooms. Within the building was a twenty-four-bed memory care unit that remained locked at all times.

The memory care unit was self-contained with a dining room, large common area, kitchen, and an outdoor space that was walled with Plexiglas so as not to obstruct the magnificent views. This unit tended to stay full, and as it should be, residents on the ALF side were given preference for admission into the unit as space became available. Joan was second on the list, so if the family said no to the open bed it would be Joan's.

We discussed our options. Neither of Sean's parents could be left alone. There was a possibility that a bed at the hospice care center might open soon, but that was not a possibility today. For the time being, Sean and I would stay in the apartment. We didn't see any other option. Sean could not leave, and I wasn't going to leave him alone to face what was coming. We were in it together.

It was up to Sean to decide what would happen. It was hard to watch. Everything he had worked to put into motion had fallen apart. His parents would not get to enjoy the spectacular views, and his father was only slightly aware of where he was. His mother was completely unaware of what was happening around her. In the course of a week, Sean had gone from son to caregiver to both of his parents. There was a sliver of hope that Joan might be able to move into the memory care unit, but it was out of our hands and we had to wait for a decision.

When the director stood to leave, he said good-bye to Joan. She walked up with a huge smile on her face. She was wearing three pairs of glasses: hers, Henry's, and Sean's. They were all balanced on the bridge of her nose. I saw that she had added my watch to her wrist and added a few shirts as well. She was happy, though, and bid Robert good-bye. Shortly after that, it was my turn to take her to the dining room. We left a few pairs of glasses behind, but we went down with multiple watches and shirts.

When we got to the dining room, people were in all stages of dinner. Some were done, some were eating, and there were many tables that had not been used yet. I picked one close to the elevator, and we sat down. I chose ham for both of us, and we settled in to wait. Dinner came quickly, and I knew right away that Joan was feeling the chaos from upstairs.

She had a very difficult time eating. She would chew something and then take it out of her mouth and line the edge of her plate with it. The ham ended up all over the table in little pieces. She buttered her roll at least five times. I attempted to start a conversation, but it was unsuccessful. She was too distracted by her dinner. I felt someone standing next to me and turned to find the nurse standing there.

She said, "It's okay that you are sitting here now, but no one sits at *that* table over there, so tomorrow that is where you will sit." She pointed to an empty table a few rows away. I stared at her and finally said, "Fine." She explained how territorial the patients were about tables and that we would make two little ladies very upset by eating there. She wanted to engage me in a conversation or debate about tables, and I wasn't biting. She stood there a few minutes more while I ate and Joan decorated her plate. It was uncomfortable, and that pretty much set the tone between the ALF nurse and me. We did not click.

The nurse finally left, and Joan finished with her food. She didn't eat much of it, but said she was done. I left the dining room thinking that I didn't want to go there again. I could see the other residents watching Joan and commenting on her behavior at the table. I didn't want anyone laughing at her. Or pointing at her. She really struggled with that meal, and I prayed that a bed would open in the memory care unit so she would be in a setting with people who had similar struggles.

When we got upstairs, the twin bed had been delivered and was positioned near the door. When lying on the bed, there was a clear view of the bathroom, and the door knob to the hallway was less than a foot from your head. That turned out to be an optimal position. Sleeping right next to the door helped prevent 1:30 a.m. escapes into the hallway.

Joan watched a little TV and looked at photos and her Ronald Reagan magazine. Henry was moving around a lot in the bed and needed to be repositioned frequently. He also wanted the urinal quite often, but he was not producing much urine. Once he knew he had a diaper on, he said, "Well, it's about time." We had the same thought. A diaper would have been really helpful in the car, but it wasn't something we had even considered.

I wanted to go home, unpack, and start some laundry. I told Sean I needed about ninety minutes at home. I walked out to my car and noticed that my bumper was not where it used to be—someone had scraped the back passenger side with enough force to pop the bumper out of alignment. No note, no apology…just several hundred dollars of damage. I went back in to ask if anyone had reported hitting my car and maybe left a note with the desk.

No such luck. Whoever drove into the side of my car did not feel compelled to tell me or take responsibility for an expensive mistake. You couldn't miss it—my car is black, and there were large white scratches in four separate areas. Robert heard what had happened and came out to take a look. We walked around the lot, inspecting the white cars for big black smudges, but we had no luck. I never found out who did that to my car.

I went home, started a load of laundry, and packed an overnight bag. I opened my mail and tried to straighten the house. We had generated several loads of laundry the night before, and I lined it up for my next trip home. I had what I needed and headed back in time to take Joan for a walk to the lobby to see a magnificent twilight view of the mountains. She wasn't that interested, but I found it very peaceful.

Early that evening, the suppository did its magic and there was a major clean-up needed. Sean and I turned Henry onto his side so I could remove the diaper and clean him up. As I pulled the diaper aside and turned back to start wiping, Sean said, "Can you get that out of my face?" The smell was bothering him, and he wanted me to move the diaper off the bed so it would be out of direct view.

I had a strong reaction to that request, with my first thought being, "Suck it up and start wiping." I was on the work side of the diaper, using the old diaper as a holder for the wipes. That's what I had learned to do as a nurse. It contains the mess and saves time. Sean was more focused on his reaction to the process than the immediate task at hand. It did not smell good; I'll give him that.

I said, not very nicely, "Just because I am a nurse does not mean I enjoy doing this. I am doing it because it has to be done. I'm a little busy." I finished cleaning Henry's buttocks, and we got a clean diaper on him. I moved the mess into a plastic bag, and we repositioned him, got him as comfortable as we could, and I gave him pain medication. He stopped me after one dropper full of Pedialyte.

Sean took the garbage bag out of the apartment. I washed my hands and started collecting plastic bags to use as waste bags. I set up a little diaper station with wipes, gloves, and plastic bags. When I came out of the bedroom, Sean told me that he had a great deal of respect for nurses and what we did. He would echo that thought when the hospice nurses visited. I think he started to see how much work it could be to be a caregiver. It's not always pretty.

It had not been a good experience for Sean, Henry, or me. When we had gotten Henry all settled and in a position he liked, he said, "I'll bet you regret bringing me out here now." We both said that wasn't the case. I said there was a learning curve with our new situation and that we were doing the best we could. I was sorry he had to hear Sean and me bickering over his diaper. It was not one of our finer moments. We were all exhausted and fuses were getting short. We did not repeat that performance. For the most part, we worked together exceedingly well. It was a well-coordinated effort.

Throughout the afternoon and evening, staff members came by to introduce themselves and welcome us. Our situation was unusual, and no one knew exactly what to make of us. The overnight nurse stopped by and said that she would be making rounds early in the morning, so if I woke up and saw someone in the apartment at one or two o'clock in the morning not to be alarmed.

The nursing assistants came by to take vital signs—it was their policy to take vital signs every shift for the first few days to establish a baseline. That is logical, but hardly welcome news when you are pushing the limits of sleep deprivation and hanging on to a good attitude by a thread.

OUR FIRST NIGHT SLEEPING IN AN ALF

I prayed we would get a decent night's sleep. I inflated my air mattress and parked it right across from their bedroom door. I got Joan into a nightgown and led her into the bedroom. She briefly looked at Henry but did not say anything to him or about him. I showed her the bed and turned down the covers. She climbed right in and went to sleep. When I came out, Sean was in bed, too. I was right behind him and had just fallen asleep when I heard Henry call out for Sean. "I need the urinal, I need the urinal." Sean didn't move.

I went in to the room and reminded him that he had a diaper on but could use the urinal if he wanted to. He did. I helped him get positioned, and he urinated a very small amount. He turned down my offer of fluid and said he wasn't in pain and did not want anything to help him sleep. I fluffed his pillows and went back to bed, again hoping that a good night's sleep was coming.

It was not to be. At least not for me. Sean was sound asleep. He remained sound asleep when Joan came out shortly before midnight. She looked down at me and poked my mattress with her foot. She walked over to look at Sean and then walked toward a closet. The bathroom light was on, but she did not make the connection. She opened the closet door and pulled up her nightgown. I jumped up and pointed her to the toilet. She needed prompting to wipe, and I did the flushing. I led her back to bed and stopped by Henry's bed to help him get more comfortable before getting back on my mattress.

I was the only one awake when the nurse came in at 1:40 a.m. to check in on Joan and Henry. I looked at her, and we gave each other thumbs up. I turned over and tried to get to sleep. My air mattress is remarkably comfortable. I had used it on top of the very uncomfortable mattresses at camp just a few weeks before. What is *not* comfortable about being a forty-seven-year-old on an air mattress is getting off of it. It was on the floor, so I had to roll off it and very ungracefully get into a standing position. I did a lot of that throughout night. It would not have been a pretty sight.

Joan was up three times and needed to be guided to the bathroom, helped with wiping, and guided back to bed each time. Sean managed to sleep through all of our bathroom get-togethers— impressive if you consider that the bathroom light fell directly on his face every time the door slid open, and Joan and I talked while we were in there.

I am envious of people who can just get into bed and fall asleep. It takes me a while to do that, and it seemed like every time I was fully asleep, it was time to roll out again and help someone. At 4:00 a.m., I called out to Sean, and he didn't move. I walked over and shook him to wake him up. His father had managed to wriggle way down in the bed and his feet were hanging off the end. I couldn't pull him up in bed alone so Sean and I did it together. Joan slept through it. Sean went back to sleep.

I was still up at 5 a.m. when an ambulance pulled up in front of the building. The apartment looked out at the entrance to the ALF, and when the ambulance pulled up, its flashing lights were like a private disco in the living room. I watched the lights for a while and finally fell back asleep. I think I got a solid hour of sleep before I heard people in the hallway.

FRIDAY, JULY 29

It was 6:30 a.m., and both Joan and Henry were sleeping. To be accurate, they were both snoring. It struck me as very funny. They had been up on and off all night, and now that it was morning they were sawing logs.

Sean went hunting for coffee, and I packed up my bed. I had commandeered one of the living room closets to store pillows, blankets, the mattress, and some clothes. I had learned that leaving things in the bathroom was not a good idea, so I kept all of my stuff in that closet. Sean preferred keeping his things zipped up in his backpack.

I wanted to shower at home, so we agreed that I would take an hour or so. Sean asked a staff member to bring up Cheerios and raspberry yogurt for his mom. When I returned, he would take some time to go home and run errands. This was our approach to staying sane. We would take turns leaving to get a few minutes of quiet.

While I was home, I took a shower, did more laundry, and made a few calls. I went into the bathroom to brush my teeth. My toothbrush didn't move when I reached over to take it out of the coffee mug I keep it in. I picked up the mug, looked inside, and burst out laughing.

The end of my toothbrush was buried in a huge wad of gum. Have I mentioned that Joan likes gum? She had apparently found the candy dish that contained gum and had used a pack as an anchor for my toothbrush. I will never know how she thought of that, but it was well-executed and effective. It was time for a new toothbrush anyway...

I left the house and walked down to a bakery to get breakfast sandwiches for Sean and me. It was blessedly quiet there and smelled wonderful. It was a welcome five-minute break before heading back to the ALF. I made a quick trip back to my house to rip out a page from my yellow pages: crematoriums. When I got back, Joan was dressed and had already eaten. That didn't stop her from admiring Sean's sandwich, and she ate half of it. I gave Sean part of mine, and we ate a quick breakfast.

I checked on Henry. He was answering questions and trying to help when I repositioned him. He liked to grab onto the side rails. Sean and I got him comfortably settled, and he went back to sleep. Sean headed out for his getaway. I had thought of a few things we needed in order to adapt to Henry's changing situation, so Sean added them to his to-do list. I gave him the page I had torn out of my phone book and told him what I had learned the day before. I was thinking it would be good to deal with that before he absolutely had to. It would be one less thing he had to deal with when his father passed.

Joan and I watched Regis and Kelly. I made frequent checks on Henry and tried to get fluid in him one dropper at a time. Most of the time he said no. He had very little pain, which was quite a blessing. His cancer had metastasized to his ribs, and I had expected him to be in significant pain. Maybe he had a very high tolerance, or maybe he was just really lucky. I am so glad he never had the excruciating pain I had seen in other patients I had cared for.

The hospice physician was planning to make a house call to examine Henry. Sean had already set up appointments with a local physician to establish primary care for both parents, but it was clear that Henry would not need a physician outside of hospice. In addition to the doctor, a social worker and Henry's primary nurse would be coming by for the case conference.

I hoped to get some information about the care center and the possibility of moving Henry there. The hospice nurse the day before had told me about the center, and it sounded like a good option. Sean was not very interested in it because he wanted to keep his parents together.

It was lunchtime and a staff member took Joan down to the dining room. We had made arrangements for her to go directly from lunch to the beauty parlor to have her hair done, so we had almost two hours for the hospice meeting.

HOSPICE

The social worker arrived first. Introductions were made, and she asked to meet with Henry for a few minutes. I brought her into the room and introduced her to Henry, who was awake and talking. I left them alone and went back to the living room. The physician was next to arrive, and he examined Henry. Right as he finished his exam, the nurse arrived, and we all sat down to talk.

I asked the physician what medications I should still be giving Henry. As the end was approaching, it didn't make sense to be giving him all of his medication. The doctor went through the list with me, and we pared it down from twelve to two. It was really nice to have a physician's opinion and another nurse to talk to.

Sean and I both wanted an idea of how long Henry could be expected to survive. He wasn't eating, had minimal fluid intake, and was mostly sleeping. That is an impossible question, of course, as no one knows for sure when death will come. The physician said we were looking at days to weeks, not weeks to months.

I was thinking days, and I think Sean was as well. The decline had been so precipitous that we had no reason to think the end would be any different. Before leaving, the doctor also offered the opinion that perhaps the stress of the drive had contributed to his current state and that he might recover to some degree. That statement did some damage to Sean's psyche.

After the doctor left, the social worker, nurse, Sean, and I talked about our situation. The social worker asked how I fit into the picture. Was I a daughter? A girlfriend? Sean spoke up and said, "She is a friend of the family." I wanted to crawl into the fetal position and cry. A friend of the family? I swallowed my pride, bit my tongue, and concentrated on the conversation. I would let my anger boil over later, but for now I needed to focus.

What was obvious to everyone was that the situation was far beyond anything we had anticipated or prepared for. Both parents needed attention, and it was not something that one or even two people could handle for any period of time. The situation was incredibly stressful. There were no beds open for Henry at the care center right now, but there might be an opening early the following week. That seemed like a long time away. In the meantime, there were possibilities for Joan that could be explored.

The ALF had a sister facility in the next town that specialized in memory care. That facility had an available bed, and Robert had already spoken to them about the possibility of Joan staying there until a bed opened in the memory care downstairs. Sean did not seem to like that idea, wanting to keep his parents together. The social worker very diplomatically and nicely said that we simply could not fight two battles at once and something had to give.

Sean was very shaken by the doctor's opinion that the trip might have contributed to the decline. He took the statement to heart and became tearful when he said he hoped he had not failed his father by bringing him here. He had not considered that the trip might be the problem.

I was, and still am, adamantly opposed to this idea. Henry's decline started before we left Wisconsin, and by agreeing to take this road trip, Sean had honored his father's last request. His father had turned down every idea other than driving, and it was his choice and clear desire to make the trip.

I spoke up right away and told Sean he had not hastened his father's death; he had done all he could to make his father's wishes a reality. During the last day of our drive, his father kept asking if we were in Washington yet. He wanted to get here and see his wife settled, and we had done exactly that. The price of his choice was that he did not get to enjoy Washington, but I firmly believe he knew we had made it and heard us when we said Joan was safe and happy.

I steered the conversation back to the possibility of Joan staying at the sister facility. I knew I was coming on a little too strong when the social worker said, "Nice job of getting us focused back on the topic at hand." I was pushing the subject because I wanted Sean to have lots of support as he made these huge choices. I told him that if he would consider at least looking at the sister facility, I would stay with his parents.

The nurse and I then went into the bedroom so she could do her assessment of Henry. That gave Sean and the social worker time to talk in privacy.

The nurse did a thorough head-to-toe assessment. When she got to his abdomen, she noticed something odd. There was a dome-shaped mass right below and to the right of his belly button. It was about the size of a grapefruit. Henry said it did not hurt when we pressed on it. It had definite edges, did not move, and was smooth. Neither of us knew what it was. The nurse said it could possibly be a tumor, but that the speed of its appearance made that unlikely. As Henry had had a repair of an abdominal aneurysm a few months before, that was also a possibility. It was strange, and she asked me to keep an eye on it.

Henry was talkative when the nurse and I were there. After she left, I asked if he was in any pain. He said he wouldn't say no to morphine. I gave him some and rearranged his pillows and blankets to make him as comfortable as I could. He turned down even a dropper of fluid. Joan was back from the salon and was pretty agitated. She didn't know who the social worker or nurse was, did not recognize her husband, and did not feel comfortable in the apartment. I took her for a short walk, and when we came back, Sean left to look at the other ALF.

WAITING AND WONDERING

The afternoon passed slowly. Henry was not comfortable but refused anything I offered. Joan wanted to leave, but I could not leave Henry alone. We took very short trips down the hall to the lobby, watched a little TV, and looked at photographs. Whenever Henry moaned or cried out for the urinal, she looked distressed. She did not understand what was happening or who was lying in the hospital bed. She did a lot of pacing in the living room and moved things around a lot. Even Ronald Reagan failed me that afternoon. She was unsettled, and I did not know how to help her.

She showed her distress with loss of function. She could not figure out how to sit on the toilet or what toilet paper was for. She got frustrated when I tried prompting her. She tried to use the shower chair as a toilet and really got irritated with me when I suggested that she pull her pants down before peeing. We kind of got back on track when I put toothpaste on her toothbrush and asked if she was ready to brush. She is an excellent brusher and spent a good ten minutes doing exactly that.

Later that afternoon, Robert came by and the look on his face told me it wasn't the news we were hoping for. The other family had decided to move their mother into memory care so there wasn't an opening for Joan. He again told me that the sister facility had openings, and if Sean felt comfortable with it, they would make the transfers as easy as possible. I have to admire the level of interest they took in Joan and Henry. I know they wanted to make them as comfortable and welcome as possible.

Joan really took a shine to Robert. She walked right up and smiled at him. He asked her a few questions but was unable to get a conversation started. She wasn't tracking very well and was having difficulty putting a sentence together. She was speaking in disjointed fragments, and I found myself wanting to finish her sentences for her. Unfortunately, I had no idea what she was trying to say.

Sean got back right before dinner. He said the PR guy who gave him a tour had been very nice and was willing to work out a respite type of admission at a daily rate that was a very good deal in comparison to a flat monthly rate. Ours was an unusual situation, and the company was trying to find a workable solution for us. Sean wanted to think about it. I was ready and anxious for a break.

An Atypical Friday Evening

Friday was fish and chips in the dining room, and I gladly handed dinner duty to Sean. I avoid seafood for the most part. I thought that a PB&J sounded great and waited to eat until I went home for my evening break. I needed to talk with my mom. I'm sure that lack of sleep and stress was contributing to my mood, but I was really upset over the "friend of the family" introduction.

I called my mom after putting in another load of laundry and told her about the day. When I said that Sean had introduced me to the hospice staff as a friend of the family, she said, "A friend of the family? Oh no, I am so sorry. That must have really hurt." As soon as she said that, I started crying. I was glad she understood why that had upset me. I was much more than a friend of the family, and it had sounded more than a little dismissive when he said it.

I had moved to Washington to share my life with him, and we had lived together for more than a year and a half. I had poured my heart and soul into our relationship, giving more of myself to him than I had to any other man. I had put my life on hold to help him make this move, and he introduced me as a friend of the family? It may have been an overreaction fueled by the situation, but it hurt just the same. It hurt very deeply.

I had a good cry, enjoyed a PB&J, and went back to the ALF. I decided to be strategic in my mattress placement that evening. Instead of putting my bed right in the line of sight for their bedroom and en route to the bathroom, I set up in front of the TV and under the living room window. It gave me a little privacy. Even better, it put Sean as the most direct source of bathroom assistance.

It was easy to get Joan ready for bed. She was all tucked in by 9 p.m., and Sean and I were right behind her. After getting Henry as comfortable as possible, we hopped into our respective beds. A staff member knocked on the door and came in to take vital signs. I asked her if she would use the ones I had just taken, and happily she did.

The staff knew I was a nurse. I think some thought I was a private duty nurse.

Once the staff member left, I climbed onto my mattress and wriggled around until I was comfortable. It crossed my mind that I was forty-seven years old and living in an ALF. That struck me as really funny, and I started laughing.

"What's so funny? Sean asked.

"Think about it, Sean. We are forty-seven years old and living in an ALF. We used to talk about growing old together, and here we are sharing a one-bedroom apartment with a bunch of eighty-year-olds. Now we know what it will be like."

"Good practice, huh?"

I must have been punchy, because I just kept laughing quietly. Sean heard me, and he laughed because I was laughing. It felt good to laugh.

By 2:00 a.m., I was no longer laughing. I had been up once for Henry and once for Joan. I heard Joan walk out of the bedroom but was only half awake. She made it all the way to the front door and was walking out when I finally woke up all the way. The light from the hall was really bright, and she was looking both directions as if trying to decide which way she wanted to go. I woke Sean when I called out to stop Joan from leaving.

She needed to use the bathroom. She had quite a bit of gas and had a bowel movement. She stood to pull up her underwear before wiping and was very confused when we tried to help. Sean was trying to keep her from pulling her underwear up, and she was tugging at it. I tried to use the baby wipes to clean her. The wiping caused her to start pooping, and Sean kept saying, "She's not clean, she's not clean." He was distressed, Joan was distressed, and I was just plain cranky. I snapped at him, saying, "She is going as I am wiping, so of course the wipes aren't clean. I'm doing the best I can."

We finally got through our little drama and got her hands washed. She went right back to bed. Henry had heard us in the bathroom and was now awake. He had a habit of wiggling down to the bottom of the bed until his feet hung off the end and he needed to be pulled back up in the bed. He told us he wanted to stand up and was not happy when we told him we couldn't do that safely. We did the best we could to make him comfortable and then went back to bed.

Sean and I didn't speak as we headed to our respective beds. A few minutes later, he said, very softly, "Nice catch with the door." I took that as an apology. I told him we would get through it and that he was doing a good thing. We both said I love you. That was something we said often. Hard to believe, but it was still true.

The fact that he had hurt me deeply by judging me in a way I felt was unfair did not change our history. He was still the man who had met my eyes through the practice room windows, kissed me at a graduation party, and wrote the poem that cemented his place in my heart. If I had walked away from him because of recent events, I would have been left with a huge hole in my heart. I had chosen to work through the pain because he was worth it. *We* were worth it.

I wish I could say I slept straight through until morning, but that wasn't the case. Henry was calling out for the urinal more frequently. He could not get comfortable but did not want anything for pain. He finally allowed me to give him something for sleep at around 3:30 a.m. Joan was up at 4:15 for another round in the bathroom. When she was finished, she walked over to Sean's bed and straightened his sheets. He didn't move. I once again marveled at his ability to sleep and cursed him for the same.

SATURDAY

It was Saturday morning. Sean found the coffee, and I got Joan dressed. I asked him what he was thinking about for his mom. I think the events of our night had helped him see that trying to care for both of them round the clock simply wasn't possible. He was almost ready to make a decision but wanted to keep thinking. None of his options were ideal, so he had to pick the one he felt was most acceptable.

I took a quick shower and went downstairs to collect Joan's breakfast of Cheerios, raspberry yogurt, cranberry juice, and coffee. It was easier for us to serve breakfast upstairs. I think Joan would have liked going down to the dining room, but that would spread us out, and we were in basic survival mode.

Once I got Joan settled at the table with her breakfast, I went in to see how Henry was doing. I was concerned about the dome in his abdomen. I had checked it a few times during the night, and it was definitely bigger. It was now the size of a cantaloupe. It was not painful, and I did not know what it was. It's hard to judge the seriousness of something when you don't know what you are looking at. While I was checking him and taking a set of vital signs, he surprised me by asking for juice.

I made a new batch of mixed berry Pedialyte and gave him a dropper full. He grabbed at the dropper and wanted more. I gave him another dropper and then a third. Three droppers of fluid is the equivalent of a tablespoon. For Henry, it was a lot to drink. We did mouth care with orange Listerine, and I put more Chapstick on him. He refused pain medication and said he was comfortable. I left the room thinking we were off to a good start.

Sean and I were sitting at the dining room table with Joan when we heard Henry gag and start coughing. He called out for his puke bucket, but it was too late. He had started vomiting and could not get the emesis basin we had positioned right by his face into position.

I ran to him and tried to steady the basin. He had thrown up far more than that tablespoon. As I tried to wipe his face, I caught a corner of mucus in his mouth. I eventually pulled out a foot-long string of coffee-colored mucus that smelled really bad and looked like a long piece of taffy. Sean had come in right behind me, but when that string started coming out of Henry's mouth, he turned around and left the room.

The linens needed to be changed, and there was vomit on the floor. I dropped a towel onto the floor to cover the puddle on the carpet and used a towel to give him a dry surface to rest on until I could get the sheets changed. It was going to take more than just Sean and I, so we asked the ALF staff if they could come as soon as they were able to help us. I prepared the sheets and got ready. The hospice nurse had arranged for the delivery of a memory foam mattress topper, and this was the perfect time to put it on the bed. We would put the topper under him when we changed the sheets.

When I went to the sink to wash my hands, Sean told me again how much respect he had for nurses and what we did.

"Just remember this when my parents go off the deep end," I said, half joking.

"Remind me to run screaming in the opposite direction," he responded, and I suspected he was more than half joking.

It was nice to hear what he said about nurses, but at the same time I wanted to explain that being a nurse does not mean you are good at every type of nursing. I had done hospice nursing for children over a decade ago, but end-of-life care for an adult was way outside my comfort zone. I decided I needed to call in reinforcements.

While Sean and I were talking at the sink, his mother went in the bedroom and started cleaning. She had picked up the towel that was covering the vomit on the carpet. I ran back in and tried in vain to keep her from sticking her hands in it. I was too late; she was wiping away at the spot with her bare hands. I put a new towel on the floor, and she went straight for it. She was also trying to pull the towel out from under his head and straighten the bedding. Henry was saying, "Leave it alone, Joan. Stop it." Joan walked to the foot of the bed and pointed at Henry, stating loudly and clearly, "He looks pathetic." She turned and left the room.

The ALF staff person came, and we changed the linens under Henry by rolling him from side to side. He was distressed and fearful we would let him roll out of bed. His agitation was growing, and he was getting angry. We got clean sheets on the bed, changed his diaper, cleaned him up thoroughly, and got him settled back into a comfortable position with the puke bucket in easy reach. While we were rolling him side to side and trying to calm him, Joan came back in and tried to clean the floor. In trying to clean Henry, position him, and not step on Joan, I wrenched my back and pain shot through me.

We thanked the staff person and left Henry after giving him some pain medication and one dropper of fluid. I walked into the living room and pressed the small of my back into the wall. The pain brought tears to my eyes, and I was trying not to lose it. Sean came over to see what was wrong. I simply said I had hurt my back.

He had seen me in pain many times before. I had been involved in three car accidents in a thirteen-month time span a few years before, and the recovery was quite painful. I went through several months when I had a very hard time sleeping. It was rare for me to get more than an hour at a time before waking in pain. During those months, I often called Sean, who would put down the phone and play his keyboards for me. The sound, and our connection, helped me relax. On more than a few occasions, he had played until I was asleep. I would wake to find the phone next to me on the pillow.

When I visited him in Washington during that time period, he would simply hug me and let me cry when the pain flared up. On this particular day, however, a hug would have been too painful. I took some Advil and called hospice.

I explained that I was unable to figure out what the mass in Henry's abdomen was and that I was concerned with its growth. He was getting agitated, and I needed some input. He was still urinating small amounts, was not constipated, and had bowel sounds. The nurse I spoke with said she would have the field nurse call me. That nurse called back almost immediately, and I described the dome-shaped mass again. After asking questions and not coming up with an explanation of her own, she said she would come out to take a look. She could be at the ALF in about ninety minutes.

I joined Sean on the couch, and we just stared at each other. I don't think we spoke at all for ten or fifteen minutes. He finally broke the silence.

"I think I should take Mom to the other place."

"I think that is the best option we have, Sean. It is temporary, and as long as we know she will get the first bed that opens here, I don't see what other choice we have right now. It's not going to get any easier."

"I'll give them a call and let them know I'll bring her after supper."

"I know you don't want to split them up, Sean. I understand that. None of our choices are good. You are in a no-win situation."

"I couldn't do this without you, Beanie."

While we were making plans, Henry started yelling, "Help me! Help me! Why don't you help me?"

Sean ran in, and his father said, "I want to know how much money I have in my wallet."

Sean said, "A few hundred, Dad. It's nothing to worry about. We have everything we need."

"I want to see it."

Sean got the wallet and counted out the bills for his father.

"How much money is in my checking account? Tell me how much."

Sean told him.

Henry said he needed the urinal and then out of the blue started saying, "Mix, mix." Sean didn't understand, and neither did I.

Angrily, Henry yelled at us, "Make me some pancakes. Why doesn't anyone listen to me? Make me a pancake, dammit!"

Joan walked by and said, "Tisk, tisk, tisk." We were baffled. I asked Henry if he was hungry, and he said no. I asked if he would try a little fluid, and he said yes to a peach smoothie. One dropper lasted about five minutes before he threw up again. I looked at the clock. It was only 10:30 a.m. Sean decided to take his mom down to memory care and ask to have her stay there until after lunch. They graciously said yes.

When Sean came back, I said I needed to go home for a few minutes to get a change of clothes and an ice pack for my back. I knew the hospice nurse was coming, and I promised to be back before she arrived. I really wanted to talk with her. I had questions about feeding someone who throws up after a teaspoon of fluid, what she thought that dome was, and what else we could be doing to make Henry comfortable.

I ran a few quick errands and came back just as the nurse arrived. We walked in together, and she was very supportive. Henry had calmed down and was able to answer a few questions. I showed the nurse his abdomen, and her eyebrows went up. She touched it, pushed it, and listened to it. She asked Henry if it was tender and he said, "Just a little bit." The nurse looked at me and said, "Well, I'm stumped. I don't know what it is."

An obvious possibility was that it could be the bladder, but that was not at all typical. When he had difficulty urinating, I had applied pressure to his bladder to see if that would help. It didn't, and he had been peeing in small amounts ever since we moved into the ALF. The nurse agreed that she did not think it was the bladder, but she offered to catheterize him just to be certain. She thought if she called the doctor that would be the first thing he asked, so we asked Henry if we could check his bladder for urine. He said okay.

The nurse inserted the catheter, and urine started flowing. It was his bladder. It had been distending for the past twenty-four hours. It didn't look like any distended bladder I had ever seen in twenty-five years of nursing, but sure enough, he needed to pee. I felt terrible. I was relieved there was an answer, but guilt-ridden that I hadn't figured it out sooner.

The hospice nurse told me it didn't look like anything she had seen before. I don't know if she said that to make me feel better, or because it was such an odd presentation, but I am grateful she said that. I asked her if there was anything I should be doing, and she said we were doing a good job. The catheter was left in place so his bladder would not distend again. I felt much better after her visit.

I asked her about his request for pancakes. I didn't want to make him sick, but I also did not want to ignore a request. She said that most of the time a person would just get the idea of a taste in their mind and take no more than a bite. She suggested that the next time he ask for something, we make a serving but offer a bite and see what happened. In her words, "Worst case is you'll have to eat some pancakes." It made sense. Strangely enough, he never mentioned pancakes again.

TOUGH DECISIONS

It was Sean's turn to go out into the real world for a while. He said he would bring back lunch. He asked me what I was in the mood for, and I couldn't think of a thing. I sat there trying to figure out what I wanted to eat and tears started rolling down my cheeks. I told him not to worry about it. I was really tired and focusing every ounce of energy and attention I had on Joan and Henry. Trying to make a decision about a restaurant was too hard.

While Sean can sleep through commotion, I have the gift of tears. I cry when I am angry, frustrated, or exhausted. It helps like nothing else can. One thing I hope I taught Sean when we were together was that tears were not always about him and that sometimes when a woman cries it is because she chooses to. They were mine, and I needed them. On this particular day, he understood and just patted my knee before getting up to go.

He suggested Chinese and headed out. One of his stops was going to be at the sister facility to do the admission paperwork. I started collecting Joan's belongings. I had brought permanent markers from my house and started labeling her clothing. I wanted to make the move as easy on Sean as I could. I wrote her name on every item of clothing and packed them in her big rolling suitcase. I put her picture books, photo album, and angel figurine on top. Ronald Reagan was carefully zipped into an outer compartment. I collected her toiletries and labeled them as well.

I checked on Henry frequently and sat at his bedside when he was awake.

"Are we in Washington?" he asked.

"We made it, Henry. We're in Washington, and Joan is fine."

"Where is she?"

"She is in the memory care unit. She really likes it there, and Sean and I both think it is a really good place."

"Good."

"Sean is going to protect her and make sure she is safe and happy. I'll help Sean in any way I can. He has lots of friends here, and everything is going to work out fine. Joan is safe."

I hoped that if he heard this enough, he would realize his work was done. He had gotten Joan to her new home and everything was okay.

"Is it time to go?"

"Where are you going?"

"Heaven, I hope."

"I think it is up to you to decide when it is time to go, Henry."

"Yeah, I know."

He took a few teaspoons of water and said yes to Chapstick. I fluffed his pillow, and when he said he needed the urinal, I reminded him that he had a catheter in place.

"Oh goody."

I agreed, and we both smiled.

As I started to leave the bedroom, he asked if the rent check had been mailed. I wasn't able to answer but said I would be sure to check with Sean when he returned. Sean had spent quite a bit of time going over finances in the week or so before we left Wisconsin, and I knew he was trying very hard to help manage his parent's money. Henry had held onto the financial reins and refused to divulge the details until the very end. That made it really difficult for Sean. Everything had to be done in a hurry.

Henry was quiet when Sean returned with teriyaki chicken from our favorite Chinese restaurant. He had also gotten an order of chicken with asparagus, and it was wonderful. A quick lunch did wonders for my spirits. It was a meal we had shared many times before, and it almost felt normal. We had a few minutes to sit down and enjoy a meal together. I went down to pick up Joan, and he started making calls about cremation services.

When I arrived in memory care, I saw Joan sitting with a few other ladies. They were talking with each other, but I had no idea what the topic was. It made sense to them, though, and she looked content. She had managed to add a watch and an extra pair of glasses, which were carefully placed on top of her own. She smiled at me through both pairs of glasses and wiggled her fingers in my direction. It was something she did in greeting. She held her hands out toward you and wiggled all of her fingers. It was her own special hello.

I asked her if she would take a walk with me, and she took my outstretched hand. We walked down the hall and out the front door to smell the flowers we had admired from her living room window. She noticed every single weed and said, "Someone better get this cleaned up before it's, you know, all messy and such and such." She recognized her car parked out front and was not at all impressed by the car next to it. It appeared to have mold growing on its sides, and she said it looked just awful. I had to agree. We spent a few minutes outside, and then went back to the apartment.

In the time we had been gone, Sean had finished his calls and chosen a company to handle the cremation. I said it was one more thing checked off on the list. We had started referring to this list when we talked about everything that needed to be done. One thing I had put on the list was to pick up a soft blanket and a larger pillow to help keep Henry in position. He was wearing just a T-shirt and socks at this point, and I wanted him to have something soft on his skin.

I had time for a run to Walmart before Sean and Joan needed to leave, so I grabbed my purse and headed out to my car. I had made the mistake of leaving my purse on the floor, though, and my keys and wallet were no longer in it. I did have plenty of new and wadded tissues, though, so I was well prepared for a sneezing emergency. I found the keys in the bathroom and my wallet in her underwear drawer. I was ready to shop.

It seemed like every day there was a new list of things we needed. Henry's condition was changing by the hour, and Joan was reacting to the stress and tension by decompensating in her ability to function. I was on a mission to improve things for both of them as I searched the aisles for what I needed.

Joan had been wearing my pajamas for most of the trip, so I picked out some pretty cotton gowns for her. Cotton underwear is much better when hygiene is not consistent so I stocked up. I picked out a nice overstuffed pillow for Henry's back and chose blue and grey striped pillowcases. I found a really soft fleece throw that was also striped blue and gray and was pleased he would be color coordinated. I got plastic pillow protectors in case he threw up on his pillows and bought oversized aloe and lanolin wipes for a bed bath. I also found some dry mouth spray.

I found small plastic crates for storing medications and toiletries. Sprite, granola bars, apples, oranges, bananas, Jell-o cups, and flavored waters would fill up their frig. I filled a cart in less than thirty minutes and headed home to the ALF. Sean and his mom called to me from the window, and seeing the size of my score, Sean came down to help me. I was loaded with goodies. Joan liked the nightgown and started to put it on. Sprite was a good distraction, though, and I quickly labeled and packed the new gown and underwear.

A Very Bad Evening

Deciding to take his mother to the other facility was very difficult for Sean. He didn't want her to feel abandoned or alone. He wanted to keep an eye on her, and I think a part of him was still hoping she would sit by her husband's side as he slipped away. She had shown no interest in Henry, though, and when we told her he was her husband, it didn't really register. When Henry called for her, she did not respond.

In spite of all of his reservations, though, he also knew that keeping her cooped up in a one-bedroom apartment while we tended to Henry wasn't fair to her. She wasn't getting the social interaction she needed, and if things went badly with Henry, we didn't know how that would affect her. She definitely reacted to stress, and Henry could be less than gracious. The care we had to give Henry was disruptive to her. It was our hope that Joan would be safe, social, and engaged while she was in the sister facility. We also hoped it would be a very short-term solution.

I gave Joan a big hug and said I hoped she enjoyed her drive. She was smiling. She liked Sean very much, and taking a drive was something she enjoyed. I watched them get into the car and hoped for the best. Henry called for water, and I got back to work. We had a pretty active evening as he threw up every time he took a sip of water or juice, but he wanted to keep drinking. I think I took a short nap sitting next to him, and he woke me with a poke to my arm. He was thirsty. I realized I was too, and after finishing with him, I went out and grabbed flavored water. I sat on the couch and thought about the evening's sleeping arrangements.

When Sean came back, there would be two of us for Henry. I was of the opinion that things would get progressively worse and had decided to offer Sean a night at home. I thought I could get through another night there and wanted Sean to be rested as he faced his father's imminent death. I had made up my mind to tell him to go home after he got back, when there was a knock on the door.

Sean walked in. I smiled at him and then noticed he was pulling his mother's suitcase. Behind the suitcase was his mother. Joan was back. I was shocked. Sean just looked at me with a strained smile and said, "Okay, Mom, we're home. Why don't we get ready for bed?" I took the hint and rummaged in the suitcase for a nightgown. The bag looked like it had been ransacked—nothing was where I had put it a few hours before.

I got what I needed and helped her get ready in the bathroom. She was a little more scattered than usual, but it was not that bad. We had a cookie and a glass of water, and then I led her to bed. She climbed right in and said, "Nighty night." Sean had been sitting at his father's bedside, and as I passed, I gave him a quizzical look. He stood up and followed me out into the living room.

We sat down on the couch, and he shook his head. He was clearly upset. I said, "Well?" and waited for him to start talking. He said it had been terrible. Horrible. It had been a huge mistake. He never should have acted so quickly and taken his mother to a place like that.

When they arrived at the sister facility, they had been shown to Joan's room, which he said was really nice. Sean unpacked all of her things and told his mom this was going to be her room for a little while. They spent some time in the room and then joined other residents for ice cream. Sean told me his mother did not seem to fit there. She was higher functioning than most of the people he saw and the residents were mostly sitting around, detached from their environment.

He was already second-guessing his decision when he walked his mom back to her room. They were accompanied by a staff person, and when they got to her room, they walked into a horror show. Someone had defecated on her bed and smeared feces all over the walls. Sean said the staff person did not seem particularly fazed by this and said they could have the room cleaned.

Sean did not do well with poop, and leaving his mother there was out of the question. He grabbed her things, threw them into the suitcase, and told his mom they were leaving. He had to go back in when he realized he had left her medication and toiletries behind, but he got out as fast as he possibly could.

He was blaming himself for making a poor choice. He felt he had failed his mother. I tried to tell him it wasn't his fault and that he had been trying to protect his mother, but I don't think he was really listening. He had already gotten a call from an executive at that facility, telling him there was a different room available. They apologized, but the damage was done, and Sean wrote off that facility forever. It was traumatic for him, and it made the memory care unit at our ALF look even better than it already did.

My good intentions about giving him a night off would have to wait, for neither of us was going anywhere that evening. Henry was calling out more frequently to ask about his wallet, his checkbook, and how much money he had. He wanted to stand up, and he was not at all happy when we told him we couldn't do that. He simply was not able to support his own weight. We offered sitting, rolling over, or raising either the head or foot of the bed. He was frustrated we could not do what he wanted.

I had put on the new pillowcases and covered him with the fleece throw and the prayer blanket. We were using the Crazy Franks pillows and the new ones I had just purchased. We really tried to help him find a comfortable position, but he just wasn't able to relax. I gave him medicine to help him sleep, and it worked for a short time.

It was Saturday night, and we were sleeping in the living room of an assisted living facility apartment. It was our own little world, and we had limited contact with our regular lives. If Sean was talking to his friends, it was when we weren't together. I was getting texts from my sister and my friend Louise. A few of the staff from camp sent messages they were praying for us. Aside from that, it was a tiny world composed of me, Sean, Joan, and Henry. The four of us lapsed into sleep.

SUNDAY

Sunday morning came far too quickly. I had been up a half-dozen times and was feeling grimy. I jumped in the shower as soon as I rolled off the mattress. I was dressed and armed with coffee when I woke Sean up at 8:00 a.m. His favorite AA meeting was Sunday mornings at 8:30 a.m., and I thought he might want or need to go. I wanted him to have support from his friends in AA. I thought they would embrace him as he faced this challenge.

He chose not to go, though. He didn't want to leave until we had a feel for how our day was going to be. He went for refills on the coffee, and I checked on his parents. They were both sleeping comfortably, and we were blessed with a few minutes of calm before the day started. We drank coffee and munched on apples. I deflated my bed and put all of my things out of view.

We agreed that breakfast in the apartment was a good idea so I went down to collect her usual. By the time I got back, Joan was sitting at the table waiting. I placed the tray down and sat next to her. She liked to mix the Cheerios and yogurt together in a bowl. She had been eating that breakfast every day for a long time. It was not uncommon for her to get stuck on the mixing step. She would stir the cereal and mash down the top of the mixture so it was flat in the bowl. She would play with the spoon for a minute and then flatten the cereal again.

It seemed that making the transition from mixing to eating was tricky. There were times I would finish my breakfast before she had started with her first bite. This was one of those mornings. She scraped the bottom of the yogurt container and mixed it with the cereal at least six times before taking a single bite. While she was doing this, Henry woke up.

He woke up worrying that he had sent out two rent checks for their house in Wisconsin. He wanted to know how many checks were left in the checkbook and how much cash was in the car. He let me give him a quick wipe-down and we did mouth care with the citrus Listerine that he liked. Chapstick was applied, and then he asked for an apple. That surprised me, but Sean cut it into little pieces and sat with him as he slowly chewed and then spit it out. The nurse had been right—he really just wanted the taste. He tried a little banana as well. He held down a few sips of fluid, and I was encouraged that we might have a good day.

It would turn out to be the most memorable day we spent with him. Although the morning started quietly, the day would not end up that way. Sean sat with him and told him that moving Joan to the other facility had not worked out. He promised she would stay right there in the apartment until a bed opened downstairs in memory care. Henry called for Joan a few times, but she did not respond. When she walked into the bedroom, he would hold out his hand and she would walk right by. It must have been very difficult for him; I think he was aware enough to know she did not recognize him.

Henry asked for his cell phone and said he wanted to make a few calls. He told Sean to get his address books out of the car. Sean came back with two address books. Henry was upset that they were not the right ones. It turned out that he had four address books. He knew some of the numbers he wanted to call, though, so as Sean sat at his side, he told him what to dial. The first call was to his niece, the one who had taken Lucky and baked the pies and dumplings for him. She was the daughter of Joan's only sister, and Henry was very fond of her.

When she got on the phone, Henry said he was calling to say good-bye. He didn't have much time left and wanted to let her know he loved her and hoped she would keep an eye on Joan. He said he appreciated all she had done for them, and would miss her. He cried, and I could hear her crying as well. After speaking to his niece, he asked to call Ally, Sean's sister.

I had overheard a conversation about Ally when we were still in Wisconsin. Henry had gone out to the porch to smoke, and his nephew was sitting with him. I was sitting with Joan at the dining room table, which was only about fifteen feet away. I could hear every word of their conversation. Henry said he was hoping to see his daughter one more time before he died.

"Do you think she'll come see you in Washington?" the nephew asked.

"Well, every year she takes off the whole month of August. She really likes spending time out on her boat, though, so I don't know if she'll make it."

Henry said this matter-of-factly and then lapsed into silence. I remember thinking how sad it was that he thought Ally would choose the boat over him. During the past six months that I had been a part of this family's changing story, there had been very little input from Sean's sister. Sean didn't understand it, and his father made excuses for it. Either way, she had chosen to be on the fringes.

Sean called his sister and told her their father wanted to say good-bye. She had not been keeping in touch very regularly since we had left Wisconsin, and I don't know if she understood how very ill he was or that he was running out of time. Those words should have told her.

The phone was handed to Henry, and he said, in effect, that he was getting ready to die and wanted to say good-bye. He said, "You were the one light of my life." My heart broke for Sean, who was sitting right next to him and hearing every word. Henry went on to tell the sister what a joy she had been and how much he loved her.

I felt myself getting angry at Henry. I knew how I would feel if I was the one sitting at his bedside. It seemed cruel that Sean was not getting the same praise from his father that was being lavished on his absent and uninvolved daughter.

I could hear most of what she was saying from the next room. She said something about her paycheck not being deposited until Monday, and then after that she would look at fares. She thought she might be able to get here on Wednesday. Henry asked what day it was, and Sean said Sunday.

"Wednesday, you think?" he asked his daughter. She said she would try to get there. He said he didn't know if he would make it until Wednesday, but he would try. If not, he wanted her to know that he loved her and would miss her. The call lasted about five minutes. Sean took the phone from Henry, who said he wanted to rest for a minute. Sean got up and walked out into the living room.

"Did I hear correctly that she said she would try to get here Wednesday?"

"That is my understanding."

"Did she really just tell your dad she had to wait for her paycheck to be deposited before getting a ticket?"

Sean just shook his head. What could he say? My anger with the sister grew a little stronger—I did not believe that the delay was due to a paycheck. If she needed help buying a ticket, Henry would have bought her one. Sean would have, too.

Earlier in the whole moving process, she had told Sean she would be available on August 18th. She had the entire month off, but when her parents were moving cross-country into an assisted living facility and her father was in a rapid decline, she was unavailable to help. I don't pretend to know her situation or what her life is like at home, but I do not understand the choices she made. The end of life is not something to be scheduled when convenient.

Henry made a few more calls to long-time friends. He thanked them for their friendship and asked them to say good-bye to others for him. The calls lasted maybe thirty minutes in total, and he was done calling.

Sean asked if I would be okay staying with his dad while he went home to take a shower. We had asked if Joan could spend part of the day in memory care, so Sean was going to walk her down to memory care and then head out for a short break. I said I would be fine.

Henry was awake, so I sat in a chair next to his bed. I fluffed the pillows a few times, gave him a few bites of apple and sips of water, and gave him pain medication when he admitted he was in pain. He seemed restless, and I started rubbing his arm to see if it would calm him. It seemed he was tying up his loose ends.

I told him that Joan was down in memory care and would be very happy there. I talked about all of the activities they had in memory care and said she would be safe, happy, and protected. I told him how proud I was of his son and that I knew Sean would watch over her and make sure she was okay. I said he had done what he wanted to do and now his job was done. We made it to Washington, Joan was happy, and he could let his son take care of things. He was free to let go.

He took my hand and told me that he and Joan had hoped Sean and I would marry. While Joan had told me that over twenty years ago, I had never heard it from Henry. He said he appreciated that I had come out to Wisconsin for his surgery and to help them get to Washington. I had not expected to hear this, and it really touched me.

We were not always sure how cognizant Henry was, but in that moment he was speaking very clearly. I held his hand and told him I would always love his son. It was quiet for a few minutes, and then he asked me a question I was totally unprepared for: "Did you ever want children?"

"Did I ever want children?" I repeated, and I heard the front door open.

"Yes, did you want to have children?"

I couldn't speak, and tears started pouring down my cheeks. I turned my head away from the doorway and tried not to fall apart. It took me a few seconds to steady myself enough to get out the one word answer: "Yes."

He squeezed my hand and my heart broke again. I had been married for twelve years to a man I loved and who loved me. For a period of time, we tried to have a child. Sometimes life turns out exactly as it should in spite of your efforts, though, and in light of the path he chose, it was a blessing we did not bring a child into the marriage. I had accepted that I would be an aunt but not a mother when Sean re-entered my life and changed my thinking.

I had wanted to have a child with the man now standing in the doorway. There was no man I would have wanted to be father of my child more than Sean, and he had talked about wanting a child as well. He had started the conversation. We had laughed about possible combinations of our physical and psychological traits. We are very different, but as Sean once put it, we fit together like the last two pieces of a convoluted puzzle. We were no longer a couple, though, and the possibility had been lost forever.

I will never know why Henry asked me that question, but it was devastating to me that it was asked and answered as Sean stood five feet away, totally unaware of what was being said. I could not stop the tears, and after a few minutes I got up and moved into the living room. Sean had picked up the Sunday paper, and I tried to focus on the coupons. He watched me for a few minutes and then said, "You seemed to be all choked up in there. What were you talking about? Wait, never mind, I don't need to know."

I couldn't have answered him if I wanted to, for the question started another flood of tears. I just shook my head. How could I explain to him that a single question could bring back the regret of missed opportunities? Or that I would have loved to have seen the child we could have created and didn't understand how his feelings for me had changed so dramatically. I was still the same person he had loved and said he wanted to grow old with. I didn't try to explain it, and he wisely let me concentrate on the coupons.

I am glad Henry and I had those few minutes to talk. It was the last time I knew for sure he was speaking to me. Things were about to go downhill, and as the day progressed, he grew more confused, agitated, and angry.

CRYING OVER PIZZA

It was time for me to take a break and get out for a few minutes. Since we had Chinese the day before, today would be pizza day. I ran by my house to pick up some paperwork and then drove to the market. It had a pizzeria inside, and it was the best we had found in our town. I ordered our usual BBQ chicken pizza with extra cheese on half and was really embarrassed when they asked if I was okay. Apparently, my recent breakdown was obvious. That, of course, started a fresh flow. I have an unlimited supply of tears.

I thanked them and assured them I was okay. I shopped while they made the pizza. I wanted to have a variety of flavors for Henry if he continued to ask for bites. Watermelon had been a big favorite of his just a week ago, so I bought that, a peach, and a variety of puddings. I got a mixed four-pack of regular and diet root beer for Sean and me. I managed to pull myself together before entering the check-out lane. I inhaled the wonderful smell of BBQ chicken pizza and calmed down. By the time I got back to the ALF, my tear ducts were off duty and I was feeling much better.

Sean told me his father was still asking about the rent checks and wondering how much money the estate sale would bring in. It wasn't scheduled until the end of the month, but it was very much on his mind. He had asked for his address books, and Sean wondered if I had moved them when rearranging the car back in Gillette. I didn't think I had, but I said I would go down to look. Henry was sleeping, so we had time to enjoy hot pizza and cold root beer.

I went to check on Henry. He was resting with his puke bucket right up by his chin. There were small pieces of apple in it, and he would put a little piece in his mouth when he wanted a taste. I told him that I had picked up watermelon, and he was happy about that. He let it melt in his mouth and swallowed the liquid. He ate more food during this day than he had in a week. He was throwing up a lot less frequently, too.

Joan joined us in the early afternoon and seemed happy. She really enjoyed the people and attention in memory care. The memory care staff had nicknamed her "the shopper." It was an accurate description and was given in an affectionate way. If she saw something she liked, she would pick it up. If it fit in her purse, it was likely to end up there. There was no malice or intent; she just shopped as she went.

I was sitting by Henry, and Sean was spending time with his mom. They were watching TV and chatting. Henry stirred and looked at me. I assured him that everything was okay. Joan was safe, and Sean was with her. He took a bite of watermelon and a sip of water. He was a little agitated, and I asked him if there was anything on his mind. He said loudly, "Yes, there is something I want to talk about."

I took his hand, thinking he was about to say something profound or wanted to talk about his wife or children. I was wrong. He said in a voice tinged with anger, "I want to know why no one will get my goddamn address book out of the damn car. That's what I want to talk about."

While we would laugh about it later, I did not find it funny at the time. Not at all. I told him we were working hard to make sure both he and Joan were well cared-for and asked what number he needed. We had his cell phone and two address books. What did he want me to look up? He did not answer with any specifics, but angrily said no one was helping him.

We tried to get Joan to sit by her husband. We were very blunt in saying, "This is your husband. He is very sick and would really like for you to hold his hand." She sat down for a moment, and he extended his hand to her, saying, "Hold my hand, Joan." She looked at his hand, looked at him, looked at us, and got back up. It wasn't registering with her, and I don't think she had any idea he was her husband and that he was dying. She returned to the living room and walked around humming. She had a beautiful voice, and I like to think that hearing her sing brought Henry some measure of peace.

Sean and I traded places. Henry asked him about the rent checks and the estate sale and how much money was in the car. Sean placed his hand on his father's chest and said, "Dad, I wish you could just let it go. It's nothing you need to worry about. We are here with you, and mom is safe." Henry replied that he was letting go, but he would continue to question Sean about the checkbook balance, number of checks left, and cash on hand.

I took Joan out to the car while I rummaged for address books. We had packed the car very tightly, and every nook was full. I retrieved bottled water, snacks, Ensure, and Boost. I even located address books number three and number four. They looked almost exactly the same as numbers one and two. I went up feeling triumphant and held them up for Sean to see. When we told Henry we had four books in total, he didn't answer us. He did not make any more phone calls.

I'll Die on Wednesday

Henry yelled that he needed help. We ran into the room, and he was frantic, telling us to turn the bed around. He was physically trying to look behind him. There was nothing there but a white wall. We asked him to relax and said, "There is nothing behind you. It is just a wall." Sean described the room and said we were in the ALF. Henry was determined to have the bed turned around. He asked where the refrigerator was and told us he needed to turn the bed around so he could see what was missing.

He wasn't in the ALF with us anymore, and we were guessing he was back in Wisconsin thinking about the estate sale. He was agitated. He grabbed my hand and said, "Joan, make them help me. Make them help me. Why won't anyone help me? Joan. Joan. Joan! Help me!" Joan never came into the room. He thought I was Joan, saying over and over, "Joan, make them help me. Turn this bed around!" I met Sean's eyes across the bed, and we tried to move the bed around.

Hospital beds are heavy, and the room was small. We managed to get the bed turned enough that he could look at the wall. It didn't help, though. He was inconsolable as he muttered about money, checks, the refrigerator, and "what is missing." It was so sad to see him exert what little energy he had on "stuff." He was hanging onto things that no longer mattered. He couldn't change their finances, and he had chosen what to leave behind. When he finally lapsed back into sleep, we left the room feeling drained.

"It's so sad," I said to Sean.

"I know. I wish he could let it go. I wish he would stop fighting."

"I think he is going to try to wait for your sister."

"I know."

Later that evening, he asked me what day it was. I told him it was Sunday the thirty-first. I once again told him we had made it to

Washington, that Joan was safe, and that Sean was going to protect her and make sure she was well cared-for. I told him that over and over again, thinking that if he believed Joan was okay he would be able to let go. He very quietly said, "I'll die on Wednesday."

THE NIGHT SHIFT

Although our world was basically the four of us, there was a constant flow of staff coming by. They checked in to see if we needed anything, to take vital signs, to do skin assessments, and to drop off sandwiches and snacks. The staff had really embraced us, and it was nice to know help was available.

It had been my intention to go home for the night, as I had to work in the morning. It was August 1, the day I told Sean I had to be back in Washington. When we first discussed the trip, we thought getting his parents moved into the ALF would be the end of the hard part. Two weeks earlier, the plan had been for Henry to be Joan's primary caregiver with assistance from the ALF staff.

There was no way of knowing that when we arrived, Henry would be on his deathbed. His rapid decline had changed everything. Joan would need a live-in roommate until a bed in memory care opened. It could be Sean, me, or someone he arranged to hire as an attendant. The apartment would never be lived in as a home—it had become a temporary holding spot.

I would not have been at all surprised if Henry passed away that evening or overnight, and I simply would not leave Sean in that position. He did not ask me to stay with him, but he seemed relieved when I offered. What was one more night in the grand scheme of things, right?

If Henry passed away in their apartment, I wanted to be there to help Sean. The day had been physically and emotionally exhausting, and the night was not likely to be any better. We spoke about how sad it was that Henry was fixated on "things." There would be no reminiscing, talking about Sean's future, or even about Joan. It was all about material things: what was missing, how much money there was, and his frequently voiced opinion that no one was helping him.

We were trying very hard to help him and keep him comfortable. Sean spent a lot of time just sitting next to him and touching his chest. We both told him that he had made it and assured him that he did not have to worry about Joan. She was going to be fine. I don't know how much he heard, though. That evening, he didn't really seem to be with us.

Sean had inflated my mattress, and we were all settled into our respective beds by 10:00 p.m. That was pretty late for Sean and me, as we are both early risers. I set the alarm on my phone and went to bed wondering how I was going to be able to refocus back on my life outside of the ALF.

It was time to settle into my new life. I had moved out of Sean's house in late April, but we hadn't established fully separate lives. Sean's frequent trips to Wisconsin, my watching his house while he was gone, our joint efforts to find a home for his parents, and my time away at camp had filled the time since we split. It was going to be a challenge to find our new boundaries.

The subject was pushed into the back of my mind when Henry called out that he wanted to get out of bed and put his feet on the floor. It was the start of another long and fragmented night. Joan was struggling to navigate the bathroom and wandered frequently. She somehow found it appealing to poke at the mattress I was sleeping on. Every evening, without fail, she woke me at least once by standing at the foot of the air mattress and poking it with her foot. She wasn't trying to get my attention; she just liked kicking the mattress.

MONDAY, AUGUST 1

I woke up as Joan walked by on her way to the bathroom. She was heading toward the front door, and I rolled off my mattress and scrambled up to intercept. Once she was settled in the bathroom, I checked on Henry. He needed to be repositioned, and he asked for water. I got three droppers of Gatorade in him. He also let me put Chapstick on his lips and provide a little Listerine mouth care.

When I walked out of the bedroom, Sean asked if I had rearranged my schedule. I didn't understand and told him that I needed to get ready to go. I looked up at the clock and realized my mistake. The phone I had used as an alarm clock was set for the wrong time zone. It was already 6:40 a.m., and I had meant to get up at 5:45 to go home and shower. Not the best way to get started on a Monday morning—it was 6:45 a.m., and I was already behind schedule.

I grabbed my purse and headed out the door. I took a very quick shower and dressed for work. I had been booked to witness and record an independent medical exam. That was something I did every once in awhile. It was my job to observe the exam and compare the written report that would be generated by the physician to what I had watched and recorded. They are never the same. I had to focus on details and pay very close attention. I was worried about my ability to do that. I was not focused on work.

Before I left for the exam, I stopped at Starbucks and got a huge caramel macchiato for Sean. I had just enough time to drop it off before heading out to meet the client. As I stood in line at Starbucks, I found myself wondering where his friends were. We had been living in the ALF since Thursday, and no one had stopped by. I didn't think anyone had even called. That was really hard for me to understand. Where was his village?

One of the reasons I had been so supportive of Sean bringing his mother out to Washington was that he had a very active base of support. He had immersed himself in AA in the two years he had been sober. Although the concept of AA is anonymity, the truth is that it is also a social network. Members know what is going on with each other, and when someone is struggling, it is well known within the community.

Sean had done plenty for members of this community. I had helped him on many occasions. I couldn't count the number of times Sean had spent his free time helping someone move, fixing something, visiting someone in the hospital, etc. He would drop whatever he was doing if he got a call from someone needing help.

I expected that his community would do the same for him. That they would surround him with support and offers to help. It had not happened, though. I had far more support than Sean did. My mother, sister, and close friends were calling, emailing, and texting. I had people to talk with. I was baffled by the fact that not one of Sean's friends had offered to bring him as much as cup of coffee or even a Sunday paper.

I had no doubt that if he had called someone and said he was stressed and thinking of drinking, a caravan would have arrived. This was a non-alcohol-related life-and-death situation, though, and the response had been absolutely nothing. I did not understand.

I kept these thoughts to myself as I dropped off the coffee and got back to work. My morning turned out really well. It was nice to turn my attention to something I was comfortable with and knew how to do. The whole process took about three and a half hours. When the exam ended, I checked my messages and saw that Sean had left me two messages.

A Big Decision

A bed had opened at the hospice care center, and the hospice nurse was at the ALF checking on Henry. Sean needed to make a decision. I asked if it was something he was comfortable with, and he said he didn't know. He was trying to decide if hospice could offer anything more than what we were doing. I told him I was on my way back and we could talk it over. I asked him to put the nurse on the phone. It was the same nurse who had visited on Friday, so she knew our situation in detail.

I asked what they could do for Henry at the care center. I wanted Sean to hear it from her. She said there would be twenty-four-hour nursing and people to provide the hands-on care that Sean and I had been struggling with. There was a place for family members to sleep and that, quite simply, it would let Sean be the son while the staff became the caregivers. She put it very well, and I hoped he was listening.

I was back at the ALF by 11:15 a.m. Joan was not there. She was spending the day in the memory care unit. The administrative staff had talked with Sean earlier that morning, and the weekend's disaster had been discussed. Understanding our current situation, they had come up with a very generous solution. They had offered to let Joan spend her days in the memory care unit while Sean cared for his father. She could stay through dinner, and then we would pick her up and take her back to the apartment. This gave us much-needed relief.

I loved Joan, and she could be an absolute delight. The level of care she needed could be exhausting, though, and both of his parents needed attention on a constant basis. I will forever be grateful for the way the ALF embraced us and found ways to make it work. Sean knew that his mother would be surrounded by people and could socialize in a safe environment.

We sat down.

"What is it that bothers you about moving your father to hospice?"

"I feel like I would be abandoning Mom, and maybe it's best to keep them together until Dad dies."

"Are you thinking your father may ask for her? Or she might be able to say good-bye?"

"Maybe. I don't know"

"Do you feel like you are failing your dad if you can't take care of him alone?"

"I can't be in two places at once."

"You don't have to be. I'll stay with your mom while you are with your dad. I'll work while she is in memory care during the day and stay with her at night. We'll make it work."

We talked for a little while, and he made the decision to accept the open bed at hospice. I would stay in the ALF at night and make sure Joan was up, clean, and dressed before she started her day in memory care. Between us, we would be able to do this.

Sean made the call to the hospice nurse, and arrangements were made to have Henry picked up at 1 p.m. I packed a small bag for him. Toiletries, all of his medication, clean socks, and T-shirts. He didn't need much. After asking Sean if it was okay, I included the eight-by-ten photo of Joan and Henry. Joan no longer identified the man in the picture as her husband, but Henry might want to see it. It went into the suitcase.

The ambulance crew arrived, and Henry was transferred onto the stretcher. He was covered with the prayer blanket and the new throw. The pillow went as well. I gave the crew a medical history and told them his wife's name was Joan and that if he asked for her or seemed awake he needed to hear she was safe and happy. I teared up while telling them that and had to fight to maintain my composure down in the parking lot.

I wanted Henry to know the goal had been accomplished. I gave him a kiss on the cheek and whispered in his ear.

"It's okay to stop fighting, Henry. Whenever you are ready, heaven is waiting for you." I said his son would be with him, and I was going to stay with Joan. I would do whatever was needed to keep her safe.

Sean was going to follow the ambulance and had packed a bag for himself. I walked over to his car and told him I was proud of him and thought he was doing the right thing. We hugged for a long time, and as they pulled away, I thought I had seen Henry for the last time.

As I walked back into the ALF, I was thinking about the changes I had seen in Sean. He had put his parent's needs first and was so very patient with his father as he watched Henry struggle to hang on to things that no longer mattered. I had watched him sit quietly by his father's side, reading as Henry slept. When Henry would stir, Sean reached over to touch his arm. When Henry was getting agitated, he would lay his hand in the middle of his chest and speak quietly to him. That seemed to calm Henry.

Sean was not a touchy-feely guy. He gave great hugs, but he was not one of those men who liked to hold hands, put his arm around you, or cuddle. He never has. He has said he didn't like to be touched for as long as I've known him. Knowing him as well I did, I was touched to see how much physical contact he gave both of his parents. He showed them they were loved with both actions and words. My friend was doing a really good job in a very difficult situation.

JUST THE TWO OF US

I went upstairs and cleaned the apartment. I put Joan's things in clear view and packed up everything that was Henry's. I wish I had been able to get the bed and oxygen picked up, but that wasn't a possibility. We would have to look at the empty bed for three days before it was picked up. I lined things up for the supply company pick-up and put anything that wasn't Joan's in a drawer. I wanted her to feel at ease and hoped that seeing her things would help.

Work was out of the question for me that day. I had brought some small jobs with me to work on while Joan was in memory care. I was having a hard time reading emails, though, and could not concentrate on anything other than our present situation. Work was going to have to wait, and I would figure out the money later. I ended up sitting on the couch eating leftover pizza and watching reruns of *Law & Order*.

I went down to memory care to have dinner with Joan. When I asked the staff if they could use an extra pair of hands, they happily put me to work. Jean was the evening shift med tech, a wonderful woman who was doing exactly what she was meant to do. She saw everything and stayed on top of all of "her people." I think her feelings about the residents were very similar to my feelings about my campers. I have tremendous respect for her. She knew a little about my background and pointed me to the table where everyone needed help eating.

I watched Joan eat from across the room. She was comfortable, and the staff gave her just enough help. I was sitting across from a delightful lady who was on a pureed diet and needed a lot of prompting to eat. We had fun. She laughed at me, and I laughed at her. She clapped her hands and said, "WOW!" for reasons I did not understand. It was really good to spend that time with the staff and residents. It felt good to accomplish something and help in even a tiny way.

After dinner, Joan and I took the scenic route through the ALF dining room because there was a soft serve ice cream machine there, and we were on the prowl for cones. She really liked ice cream cones, and so did I. It gave us something to do and kept us out of the apartment. I did not know what to expect when she saw the empty bed. I didn't know if she would even notice. There wasn't any hurry, though, so we went up to the lobby where a stereo was playing some music familiar to her.

She hummed and sang and walked around the lobby, picking up specks of paper off the carpet. I texted Sean, asking if Henry was comfortable. I got an immediate, "Yes-it is really nice here."

I texted back: "Good. You have been incredibly caring, strong, and loving in an impossible situation. I am proud of the person you have allowed yourself to be."

His response came right back: "Thanks. Can't wait to go back to being irresponsible and worried about what we're going to watch on TV." He still said "we."

My answer: "Mom and I having cones and singing in the lobby. Mom feisty but ok."

He called me a few minutes later and said the staff was great. They had done a wonderful job of cleaning Henry up, shaving him, and washing his hair. Sean said they made so many comments about getting him cleaned up that he felt we had neglected him. He said he thought maybe we should have done more. Henry looked really good now, though, and was resting. I was glad Sean liked the facility so much and hoped it made him feel good about deciding to move his dad.

Joan and I went to her apartment. She walked around the living room and then walked through the bedroom. She did not mention that Henry was gone, and I wasn't sure she even noticed. She seemed a little calmer, though. The apartment was quiet. I suggested that we clean out our purses. It was an activity we had done many times before, and it was kind of fun to see what she had collected. She had two purses to my one, but we dumped everything onto the dining room table and looked at what we had.

She had a white handkerchief. She stood up and walked into the bedroom. She very deliberately and gently laid it on the empty bed, right where the imprint of Henry's head was. She said, "I'll leave it here for Daddy," and then started looking through the dresser drawers. It was very sweet. It was the only indication I saw that she was aware that a man had been there.

We watched TV and drank soda. She had Sprite, and I had Diet Coke. It was time for her medication, which was a challenge that evening. She had three pills. I held out the pills and said it was time for her pills. She looked at me like it was the first time we had ever done this. "What? Me? Yup, yup, yup. That's okay." She would not take them, so after a few minutes, I put them in her hand and held out her Sprite. She closed her fist around the pills and drank the Sprite. I told her she still had a few pills left, and she looked puzzled.

This went on for at least fifteen minutes before she took the pills and dropped them into the open soda. That was a new move. Every night, it was a little different. It could be very frustrating, but that is a part of Joan. The more I got to know her, the more I realized that sequential steps were very hard for her. If you think about it, taking pills is a multistep process. I waited another thirty minutes and handed her new pills. She put them in her mouth and swallowed. Go figure…

I put my pajamas on and helped her into hers. We brushed our teeth together and looked through the Ronald Reagan magazine. She thought the red carpet in the White House was terrible but that Ron and Nancy looked like a happy couple. She said he had the nicest smile, and she liked when he had visited her daddy.

It was a nice evening, and by 9:00 p.m. we were both in bed. I had moved to the bed by the front door, and in order to make sure she didn't leave without my hearing her, I parked the portable oxygen tank in front of the door.

POCKET DOORS

We left the bathroom light on at night, and I slid the door almost closed because the light was shining on me. I don't think it bothered Sean, but I liked to sleep in the dark. I realized my mistake a few hours later when I woke to hear Joan doing her "Tsk, tsk, tsk" sound.

I saw her standing in front of the bathroom, trying to push the door open. When that didn't work, she tried to pull it toward her. Then she tried to poke her head through the open space. The pocket door was beyond her problem-solving ability. I let her in, and she said, "Dumb dumb door, you have to watch that dirty rat, yup, yup, yup." My fault entirely, for she had let us know about this problem before.

On our first afternoon in the ALF, she had gone into the bathroom, and I closed the door almost entirely to give her some privacy. We had a lot of traffic that day, and the bathroom was in clear view as you walked into the apartment. I heard a flush, but she did not come out. I was talking with Sean, I think, and thought she was puttering or something. A few minutes later, I looked over and saw her looking out at us. She was calm and didn't say a word. She just couldn't figure out how to work the door so she was standing there and waiting.

I don't know how long she would have waited there, but she was apparently not in a hurry. I got Sean's attention and glanced over at her. He said, "What are you doing there?" and slid the door open for her. She smiled at him and grabbed his arm, saying, "You're a good boy." It was pretty funny at the time, and I should have remembered.

I learned that evening that I could indeed sleep with the light on and the door open.

Tuesday, August 2

We had a pretty good night, and Joan slept until 7:00 a.m. I had laid her clothes out the night before, and she was going to have breakfast in memory care. One of the staff members was going to come by and get her at 7:30 a.m., so all I had to do was get her up and dressed. Our only difficulty was with her shoelaces, but we were ready right on time.

I had already heard from Sean that his dad had a pretty good night. Sean was going home to shower and would then spend the day with his dad. He was really pleased with the hospice care center, and it allowed him to just be the son. I think that was enormously important. He planned on coming to see his mom later that afternoon so she wouldn't feel left out.

I planned on going home to shower and trying to work. I still couldn't focus, though, and didn't want to do a half-hearted job. I answered all of my emails, sent out some inquiries, and gave up. I spent the day doing laundry, grocery shopping, and cleaning. I had until 6:00 p.m. to pick up Joan.

Sean called and asked if I wanted to go out for an early dinner. The idea of sitting down and being served sounded absolutely great, so we met at our favorite Italian restaurant at 4:30 p.m. For the first time in what seemed like forever, we were able to just be. We sat in that restaurant and relaxed. He told me about hospice, and I talked about my day. I told him I was having a hard time working, and he said he understood. We had a very nice hour together, and it felt good. A little shelter from the storm.

After dinner, we went to the ALF, and he picked his mom up from memory care. They took a short walk outside and came up to the apartment. I saw Sean look at the empty bed and the handkerchief placed where his father's mouth would have been. He stayed with us for a little while, then left to go see his father.

When he was with one of his parents, I think he felt like he was abandoning the other. He was in a position he never could have prepared for, and I think he was doing an admirable job. Joan and I were in our PJs shortly after he left. I got her to bed a little after 9:00 p.m., parked the oxygen tank in front of the door, and went to sleep.

WEDNESDAY, AUGUST 3

It was another restless night. Joan got up a few times. The first time, she stood at the foot of my bed and picked at the blanket, trying to smooth it out. My feet were in her way, and she could not get the blanket as smooth as she wanted. I finally got up so she could fix the blanket. After she was done, we went to the bathroom and she did pretty well on her own. I led her back into her bedroom and turned on the CD she liked to listen to.

It was hymns put to the sounds of nature, and she would hum along with the tunes until she fell asleep. Joan had a beautiful voice; she had been active in church choirs and as a member of Sweet Adelines. She remembered the words to many songs, and even if she didn't know the words, she would often sing along with the car radio or CD player. It was comforting to her hear humming in her bedroom. It helped me go back to sleep.

Sleep was never long-lasting with Joan, however. We were up for good by 6:00 a.m. that morning. It was too early for coffee so we made do with Sprite and Diet Coke. I decided to take advantage of the early hour to get her into the shower. This was an easy morning for us. Joan jumped right in and let me wash her hair. She was good with a washcloth. It was interesting to me that she was always fastidious with her toes. She washed them very carefully and dried them with equal attention. She never missed her feet.

While she was working on her toes, I texted Sean to see how their night had gone. He answered that his father had slept most of the night and seemed comfortable. He had started having seizures the night before, but the medication they were giving by an IV drip was helping with that. I texted back a simple message: "You have done right by your father. I love you." He answered, "Thanks."

Joan was ready to go to work. She seemed to be under the impression that she worked in memory care. She would help wipe the tables after meals, tried to help people in walkers and wheelchairs, and generally picked up things and put them where she believed they belonged. She also continued picking up other people's possessions and adding them to her wardrobe or purse.

We learned to check her before she left the unit at the end of the day. Sometimes, she would have a few too many pairs of glasses, excess watches, or even extra layers of clothing. She looked so sweet and innocent as she stood there draped in other people's things. It was a part of being Joan now, and we adapted to her habits.

She wasn't always shopping, though. Sometimes she gave things away. She had $3 in one of her purses, and she shared the wealth. The staff finally put it away in an envelope marked for Sean because it was hard to keep track of. On this morning, she went down to memory care in a well-matched outfit and a purse full of tissues, peppermints, and emery boards.

I dropped her off in the dining room after putting on her apron and getting her settled into her chair. The memory care used aprons instead of bibs, which I thought was much more dignified. Joan used to wear aprons in her kitchen, so she felt quite at ease putting one on. It was one of many things I appreciated about the approach in this unit.

My grandmother was in many different facilities in the last years of her life. Some looked gorgeous but offered nothing in the way of programming. Some looked okay but did nothing to engage the people staying there. One of the places she stayed at actually parked all the women in front of a TV playing Spanish-language soap operas. To the best of my knowledge, none of the ladies spoke anything other than English. The food was outstanding though.

Each place offered something positive and something negative. It was a balancing act in which no place was perfect, and your definition of what was acceptable was based on what was needed for your person. My person, Joan, needed socialization in a safe environment in which she could wander but not escape.

Another appealing aspect of this particular unit was that the entrances required that you enter a code at two entrances about fifteen feet apart. That made escape twice as challenging. The unit had soaring ceilings, murals painted on the walls, and stations set up along the hallway that allowed residents to explore areas of importance to them.

There was a travel related station, a wedding dress station, a sewing/craft station, a birdcage, a fish tank, a typewriter station, and two cradles with life-like dolls and baby clothes. When Sean and I first visited the unit, one of the residents had been holding a doll and talking to it. She looked very happy, and it was nice to see that this unit encouraged the residents to engage in whatever was important to them. Joan showed an interest in the baby clothes. Shopping was her number one activity, but she also liked the babies.

I left her that morning in the dining room and went home to shower and get to work. I continued to struggle with concentration and got very little done. I managed little other than organizing my desk and putting cases in order of priority. I had a meeting with a client at 10:00 a.m. in the town halfway between the ALF and the hospice care center. I texted Sean to see if he needed anything or wanted some company. We had taken to texting since the sound of talking on the phone seemed to irritate Henry. Texting was safe and did not disturb anyone.

LUNCH AT HOSPICE

Sean said he would like to have some company, so after meeting with my client I drove down to hospice. It was a beautiful facility, and the staff was very nice. I sat next to Henry for a few minutes. The room was beautiful, and the atmosphere was peaceful. He looked good. Clean, comfortable, and sleeping quietly. The seizures were coming every few minutes. He did not appear to be in pain, though, and I again said a quick prayer that he would never feel the pain of bone cancer.

Sean and I walked down to a little dining room that had really good soup and bread. Coffee and tea were always available as well. I was drinking a lot of coffee that week, and it was nice and strong. It turned out that several of the aides and nurses at hospice also worked at our ALF. Some knew Joan already, and many of them knew our story. When the inevitable question came about who I was and how I fit in, Sean again struggled to find an appropriate word. I introduced myself simply as "Sean's friend."

When we finished with our soup, we walked down the hall to Henry's room. Sean was in front of me. He stopped, turned around, and looked at me. There were tears in his eyes as he spoke very quietly, "Can I introduce you as my best friend?"

As he asked that question, I saw my friend from high school. I realized he didn't know where we stood any more than I did.

"Of course you can."

We stood there for a few seconds, just looking at each other. The tears in his eyes melted away layers of anger. I can't explain why it happened with those glimmers of tears, but I finally let go.

I realized that being friends was the most we ever should have been. It didn't matter that he wouldn't acknowledge the reason we split. I knew why. I couldn't change his thinking, and knowing how he saw me made a future together impossible. We had passed the point of no return and were left with the threads of a once-beautiful friendship that had to be reinvented. I was going to see this through with him and then move on.

I told him that if he didn't want to leave his father, I would pick up his sister at the shuttle stop and bring her to hospice. He said he would let me know. I had been home for about an hour when a text arrived, asking if I would pick her up. The plan was for me to bring her to hospice so she could see her father and then drive Sean to the ALF so he could pick his mom up from memory care after dinner.

If all went as planned, I would be home in my own bed for the first time in fourteen nights. I was thrilled at the thought of sleeping through the night. I got a little bit of work done and headed back to the same town where I had met with my client that morning.

I wasn't looking forward to seeing his sister. I had more than a few problems with her lack of involvement in her parent's dramatically changing lives. Having lived with Sean, I knew firsthand how detached she had been during this seven-month process. I didn't understand her actions so far and did not know what to expect.

THE SISTER

Sean's sister took a shuttle from the airport and planned to arrive at a local hotel at about 4:00 p.m. The shuttle was usually right on time, but on this day it was nowhere in sight. There was some sort of military convention going on at the hotel, and it was very crowded. Sean and I texted back and forth, and he called his sister to make sure she hadn't gotten off at the wrong stop. It turned out the shuttle was running late. It finally pulled in, and I recognized her right away. I hadn't seen her since 1988, but I knew her instantly.

We hugged and walked over to my car. She mocked my Chicago Bears license plate and told me how much she enjoyed when the Packers beat them in the conference finals the year before. She started chatting about sports. I told her we were about twenty minutes away. During the drive, she told me what a disappointment the flight crew had been. They were not as entertaining as she thought they should be, and the flight had not been enjoyable.

Ally talked about her month-long vacation. She always took off the entire month of August because she did not like the Southwestern heat. She told me she planned on cleaning out her closets when she got back home and that the rest of her vacation would be spent on her boat. She was eligible for retirement in 2 1/2 years, and the money was good. She hadn't decided what she would do after that. Sean had told her how pretty it was in Washington, and she said she might buy a vacation house. She talked the whole way to hospice. I said very little.

I gave her the opportunity to ask questions or start a conversation about the obvious topics, but she did not choose to ask anything until we pulled into the parking lot. As we pulled into a parking spot at 4:46 p.m., she asked what I thought of the place. I said that under the circumstances it was the best possible solution and that her father had gotten excellent care. She said "Good" and the conversation was over. We walked in together and signed in at the desk. It was 4:48 p.m.

I walked her to her father's room and said hello to Sean. I wanted to give them privacy and said I would wait down in lobby after getting a cup of coffee. They were hugging as I left the room. I felt like my head was going to explode and had my phone out before I got to the coffee pot. I called my mother, who I knew would share my feelings. Unfortunately for my father, she was not home and he got the brunt of it. I relayed the car conversation and asked him, "What is missing from this picture?"

My father said, "It sounds as if she never asked about you, Sean, her mom, or her dad. Wow. She didn't ask anything at all?"

I was just hanging up when Sean rounded the corner.

He sat down and asked me what the plan was. I told him my plan was to take him to his mother at the ALF. I thought he was going to spend the night with his mom, and his sister was going to stay with their father. Their father had, after all, been waiting since Sunday for her to arrive. Sean said he would be back. He returned about a minute later and said, "Ally says she is not cut out for this and wants to go see Mom." I was stunned. "Are you sure?" Sean said that is what she wanted. I told him to sit down.

I unloaded on him about the total lack of interest his sister had shown in any of us, particularly her father. There was no filter on my mouth at this point, and I told him that she was a poor excuse for a human being and I wanted nothing to do with her. When I asked him what was wrong with her, he just smiled a little and said, "That's Ally. She is who she is, and that's okay." He asked if I would drive her back to the ALF, and I said I would. I would wait in the lobby until she was ready to go.

I had just enough time to go to the bathroom and sit down on a couch when I saw them walk down the hall together. Sean looked resigned. Ally said she was ready to go. It was 5:00 p.m. I told her we didn't need to leave right away and she had at least another twenty minutes before we had to go. Sean said she wanted to go to a drive-through since she was hungry and hadn't eaten since 6:30 a.m. I looked at him, looked at her, and said fine. We walked out to the car together. I hugged Sean, and he whispered a thank you. Ally and I left hospice less than fifteen minutes after we had arrived.

The drive to the ALF was much of the same. Ally talked about herself, her son, and her possessions. She didn't ask me a single question about my life, her brother, or our recent trip. She didn't ask about the ALF where her mother was living. She didn't ask if we needed anything. I know people respond to situations differently, but the person sitting in my car was not a person I wanted to be around.

At one point, I stopped the conversation by saying, "Let me tell you about your mother." I described her current behaviors and needs. She cut me off, saying that she had worked as a nurse's aide when she was younger and knew what to do. She had visited her parents in Wisconsin for four or five days in May, so she knew all she needed to know about her mom.

Sean had joked on many occasions that his sister was the "son my father never had." I asked his sister about her son, who was in the military. She told me she had called her son after talking with Henry on Sunday. When she told him he needed to call his grandfather to say good-bye, he had responded by saying he wasn't good at things like that. Henry's only grandchild chose not to call to say good-bye.

Halfway to the ALF, we went through a Burger King drive-through. She told me what she wanted, and I ordered for her. She did not ask if I wanted anything, and I chose not to order. I planned on being back in my own house as quickly as possible. While we were waiting for our turn at the drive-through window, she showed me her badge. She works as a prison guard and is very proud of being in law enforcement. To be quite frank, I really was not interested.

I made one last stop on the way to the ALF. I asked if she would like to stop at a grocery store to pick up anything she might want to eat or drink. We were in and out quickly, and we were back at the ALF around 5:45 p.m. We had fifteen minutes before we needed to pick up Joan from memory care. We brought her suitcases up to the apartment so I could give her a quick tour before we went to get Joan.

REST IN PEACE

As we walked into the apartment, Ally's phone rang. It was Sean, telling her that Henry had died at 5:52 p.m. She said okay, hung up, and looked at me. "He *is* a stubborn old goat—he waited for me. He waited for me to tell him to let go."

I was speechless. And angry. Really angry. I believe that if she had told him on Sunday she could not get here, he would have died that day. He hung on for three long days because he wanted to see his daughter. I will always wonder what she was doing between the good-bye call on Sunday morning and her eventual arrival.

She had the chance to be at her father's bedside as he passed away. She was given the opportunity to sit by her brother and offer support. In the end, however, she opted for a Whopper Jr. with cheese, no tomato. As her father spent his last hour on earth, she was in my car telling me about her job, her bad knee, her arthritis, and the problems she had with her health insurance.

We walked together to the memory care unit to pick up Joan. Staff asked about the situation and how Henry was doing. I told them he had just passed, and they expressed condolences. Ally announced, "He waited until I got here to die. He waited for me." It was as if she was proud of that fact. That her father had held on for seventy-two hours so she could spend twelve minutes with him before asking to be taken to a drive-through for dinner.

I had an urge to hurt her. There were many things I wanted to say. I was exhausted, and my patience was hanging by a thread. I didn't say a thing, though. I had already told Sean what I thought of her and that as far as I was concerned she was on her own. It was better for both of us if there was minimal contact.

Joan saw me and gave me a big wave and a smile. I introduced her to her daughter and gave them a few minutes to chat. The three of us walked up to her apartment together. After spending a few minutes with the two of them, I kissed Joan on the forehead and told her I would see her soon. I walked out to my car and picked up my phone. I knew there would be a missed call.

I had a message from Sean. I listened to the very brief message that simply said, "Dad passed away at 5:52." He was crying as he spoke, and hearing him cry made me cry. I called him back and got voice mail. I told him I was proud of him and that I hoped he knew what a good son he had been. I drove home and sat in total and welcome silence.

He called me, and I apologized for lambasting his sister—he didn't need to hear my opinions of her. I meant every word of it, but I should have saved those thoughts for my mom. He said he would stop by on his way to the ALF. There had not been much to do at hospice, and he was already on his way back.

I called my mom and once again vented my frustration. Nearly every visit back to my apartment while I had been living in the ALF had included a call to my mom to tell her what was happening. I had an endless supply of support and encouragement from my parents, and I knew how very fortunate I was to have that. She commiserated with me and told me she was proud of what I was doing. I hung up feeling much calmer.

When Sean got to my house, he didn't come in. We simply hugged, stood together for a few minutes, and hugged again. He said he knew his father was at the end because he became quiet and calm. It was a peaceful end. I was glad Sean had been there, and I know he will be able to hold onto that. No matter how hard the journey had been, he had honored his father's request and gotten him to Washington. He had been a loving son and had the opportunity to show his father the man he had become.

I don't know if Henry ever really acknowledged these things. I don't know if he ever told Sean he was proud of him or said thank you for the extraordinary effort Sean put into the last months of his father's life. I hope Sean understands the gift he gave his father.

Sean left my house planning to go see his mother for a few minutes and then go home to sleep in his own bed. I was in my pajamas as soon as he pulled out of my driveway and soon settled comfortably in my own bed. It was so comfortable and so very quiet—no one walking in the hall, no CDs playing, and no one else breathing within hearing range. I relished the absolute quiet and slipped into a deep sleep. I don't think I moved at all that night.

BACK TO WORK

I woke up at 6:15 a.m. to the sound of seagulls. I just lay there for a while, thinking about what needed to be done. My first priority was coffee. After that, I really needed to assess my work commitments and get back to my own life to some degree. I was self-employed and got paid by the hour. I had really struggled to get anything done while I was sleeping at the ALF. It had been two weeks since I had left for Wisconsin, and I had only billed five hours.

Sean called, and we talked for a few minutes. I don't remember what we talked about, but we just wanted to talk. We had been through an unbelievable week. Henry had died on his seventh day in Washington. It felt like a year. We weren't done by a long shot, but Sean could now focus the bulk of his energy on Joan.

Ally would be staying until the following Thursday, so in essence I had a week off. I vowed to clear my head and get back to my own life as soon as possible. I had lots of work waiting for me, and I wanted to get caught up before his sister went home. I wasn't sure what was going to happen then, but I had a week to devote to the stacks of medical records sitting on my desk. Unfortunately, my mind was running in many directions, none of them involving my work.

I was trying to sort through my feelings. In many ways, I was angry at Henry. He had left behind a mess that Sean would have to sort through. I had always thought they were financially stable, but the reality was far short of security for his mother. She would probably be out of money in a year or two, and Sean would have to deal with that as well. I remember talking out loud as I washed dishes, practically yelling at Henry for the choices he had made and how it had affected us.

I managed to make plenty of phone calls that day. I talked with my mom, my sister, and my friend Louise, who had been sending texts throughout the trip. She was the director of a day program for seniors with dementia and Alzheimer's. She could really understand what I had been dealing with and could also laugh with me about the things some people wouldn't be able to appreciate.

It was Louise I had turned to after the disastrous road trip Sean and I had barely survived back in 1988. She and I had been friends since sharing an apartment right after I graduated from nursing school. She had just moved to Texas, and we met in our orientation at UTMB. It was an instant friendship.

She knew my history with Sean and offered unwavering support when things fell apart in Washington. I will always be grateful for the laughter, support, shoulder, and tears she shared with me. We laughed a lot as I recounted this journey. She could relate to everything I described because she saw it every day.

I let people know that Henry had passed away and checked in with my friends at camp. There had been sessions going on while I was making this trip with Sean, and I wanted to know how it had gone. It was becoming more and more clear to me that a few weeks of camp every year wasn't enough time with this population I loved so much. It was one of many things I was thinking about. It was Thursday—and Thursday was talent show night.

TALENT SHOWS

My absolute favorite hours at camp were Thursday evenings. We had a talent show after dinner, and those shows were the highlight of my year. I have tried explaining them to friends and family, but words fail to do it justice. The best way I can describe it is as the purest expression of joy you will ever see.

Both staff and campers got dressed up for dinner because talent night was also formal night. I took great pains to create a tiara worthy of the evening's events. There is something to be said for the simple act of wearing a tiara. It makes you feel happy and carefree. Each night of camp, I had a different headband or tiara. I wore it from dinner until my last "tent call" before going to bed. I like to think it made me more approachable to both the campers and the counselors. I also liked wearing them.

For the talent show, every camper was encouraged to take the spotlight and do whatever he or she wanted to. Some of the campers worked on their act all week. Some recruited counselors as "back up" singers or dancers, and some wrote and directed skits. The beautiful part of it was the profound lack of inhibition or shyness. It was an atmosphere of total acceptance and unlimited love and support.

My parents scheduled their visit to Washington to coincide with one of my camp sessions. I had told them how much I loved our shows, and they joined us for a Thursday evening. I was so happy to share this with them, and the campers put on a stellar show. Talents ranged from dealing a deck of cards, singing "Jesus Loves Me," tossing beanbags, a talk show, dancing, and a rousing version of Johnny Cash's "Ring of Fire." Every single performance was greeted with love and applause, and we laughed, cheered, and clapped until our hands hurt.

At the end of the evening, as with every Thursday night at camp, I was reminded of how little it really takes to bring joy. It has nothing to do with money, material things, or status. All it takes is a roomful of people offering each other what is so often lacking out in the "real world": love and acceptance of one another. Seeing the beauty inside of every single person and not judging them for their "outer shell."

My parents had commented on how involved the counselors were and how they participated wholeheartedly in skits and dancing they would probably never do outside of camp. The college-aged counselors, who come to camp with makeup, coordinated clothing, and the usual reservations about what others thought of them, learned quickly that none of those things mattered. Not at camp. Makeup was useless, for it was inner beauty that was on display. I hoped they would carry that lesson with them when camp was over.

Many years ago, I worked for an agency in New York that served adults with developmental disabilities. One of my "guys" had spent the day working at a dollar store, where the owner graciously hired our people to stock shelves. This young man returned from work saying he had a stomachache and needed to see the nurse. He came to my office, and I discovered he was upset because customers had been making fun of him. He just wanted to ask me why people were mean.

I told him I did not have a good answer to his question. Sometimes people just didn't think about what they were saying, some people acted foolishly because they didn't know any better, and sometimes people were just plain mean. I told him I hoped he knew that lots of people loved him and accepted him exactly as he was.

He asked me if anyone had ever made fun of me. My answer was an absolute yes. I have struggled with my weight throughout my life, and on many occasions I have been treated as a lesser person because of it. I told him that people had made fun of my weight, and he said something I will never forget: "I don't care if you are fat, nurse. You have lots of band-aids, you smile at everyone, and you dance real good. To me, you are beautiful." He had an IQ of sixty-two. If only we could all see each other with such clarity...

I have been humbled over and over again by the generosity of spirit that is so prevalent in this population of people. As I sat on my couch trying to make sense of everything that had happened, I found myself wishing it was talent night and I could put on my tiara.

LESSONS FROM HENRY

The Henry I traveled cross-country with was not the same Henry I remembered from my days as their house sitter and "third child." I had spent Christmas with them in Texas when I couldn't go home to Chicago for the holidays. Neither Sean nor his sister had been there that year. It was the three of us, and I remember it as a very happy time. I went shopping with Joan and Henry, and we played cards. They both liked to cook and gave me the recipes to add to my collection.

I was a poor nursing student, and they were overly generous when I would house sit and take care of their dog. They traveled a lot. I remember one time I was house sitting while they were on a cruise. Sean was no longer living with them, and they told me not to let him in the house. He was in a wild phase, and they had told him he could not come home until he straightened up. That was an impossible situation for me. I loved his parents, but this was Sean. He stayed with me almost the entire time they were gone, and while I had disobeyed his parents, we had a wonderfully fun week. Kids will be kids. Sorry, Henry.

I kept in touch with Joan and Henry through the years, but I did not see them from 1990 until 2008. In 1990, they visited Sean in Washington, DC, and we went on that dinner cruise. In September 2008, I met Sean in Dallas and we traveled together to his parent's house. His father needed surgery, and Joan was in the early stages of Alzheimer's. We were there to keep an eye on Joan as Henry was in the hospital. During the five-day trip, we had time to catch up, and Joan was still able to reminisce and tell stories. As we left, she told me she hoped some day her son and I would marry.

That wasn't the first time she had said that. When Sean and I arrived at their home at the end of our 1988 road trip from Los Angeles, I was supposed to stay for a few days. They had bought tickets for a concert and made plans. I was honest with them and said that while I loved their son, I really did not like him and needed to leave.

I remember his father saying that he had been around people who had just gotten sober and found them to be overly critical of people who were not so "self-aware." That hit the nail right on the head. Sean had given me a detailed accounting of my many flaws during our trip, and I was furious with him. Henry said he understood, and Joan said, "I wish my son would see what is standing right in front of him. We have always hoped you would be our daughter-in-law."

I had so many good memories of Joan and Henry. When Sean and I went to Wisconsin for their sixtieth anniversary, however, they were strangers to me. Henry had changed, and Joan did not recognize me. She was happy to see me, though, and took my presence in their home in stride. Henry seemed to be a different man. I think maybe his attempts to care for his wife almost totally alone had simply drained him. They had moved back to Wisconsin in 2009 to be closer to family, but by the time they got there it was almost too late.

Henry dealt with Joan's Alzheimer's by pretty much keeping her in the house. My grandfather did the same thing when my grandmother started showing more and more confusion. The problem with this approach, though, is that it makes it harder on both of them. Henry was exhausted and very frustrated by his wife's inability to do what she used to do, and Joan had limited socialization and felt Henry's impatience. He was less and less able to be patient with her, and his anger reflected in her behavior. It was a no-win situation for both of them.

During the visits to Wisconsin, I found myself wondering what had happened to the kind and generous man I remembered. Henry was critical of people and made unkind comments. He was very nice to me and told me he appreciated my coming out to "guard him," but he wasn't so nice about other people. It bothered me that I got more positive feedback than his son did. Sean had rearranged his life to help his parents, but I think I got more appreciation than he did. It wasn't fair.

I was with Henry almost around the clock for twelve of the last fourteen days of his life. There were glimmers of the man I knew, but for the most part, the man I remembered was gone. In those last days of his life, Henry showed me a path I did not want to take. The last days of his life were so very sad.

He held onto money and possessions. He was angry, frustrated, and lashing out at the people surrounding him. I watched a man worry about things that no longer mattered while his son sat at his side. It wasn't like those touching scenes you see on TV. He went out angry, and it was heartbreaking to watch. Joan did not know he was her husband and was for the most part detached from his ending. In essence, it was only Sean and I who saw this, and for that I am thankful. Others will have much happier memories of him.

Henry showed me how I did not want to die and gave me a wake-up call. I want to spend my final days on a path opposite to the one he chose. He taught me that I needed to examine my own life and make changes that would help me have a different ending. I hope that when my time comes, I will be thinking of people, happy memories, and a purposeful life. I do not want to be caught up in material things. His death made me re-examine my life. Thank you, Henry.

MY WEEKEND OFF

Friday was uneventful, and I finally got some work done. I was sitting at my desk when I heard someone making chirping noises outside of my window. It was Sean and his sister. They had been walking around the waterfront and stopped by. I wasn't thrilled he had brought Ally to my home when he was aware of my feelings, but it was a short visit and she was fine. I gave her some maps of the town and a magazine about driving tours of the state. She wanted to see the area while she was here. I told her I hoped she had a good week. They left, and I went back to work.

The next morning, Sean called and asked if I wanted to go to breakfast. You would think we would want some time apart, but we were talking quite a bit. He came to my house, and we walked down the street for breakfast. We sat at the same table we had shared before.

We had lots to talk about. He was going to start working again on Monday, and although it would be a relief to get back to his life in at least one way, he was feeling like he had a million things to do. He had to think about putting together a memorial service back in Wisconsin, notifying everyone who needed to be notified, making sure his parent's bills were paid, and trying to figure out everything that was entailed in settling his father's estate. It was understandably overwhelming.

He asked how I was doing with getting back to work, and I told him that I just didn't have the same level of excitement about my work. I had been very happy as a self-employed legal nurse consultant, but now I felt as if I should be rethinking my career. He understood. He was having similar thoughts.

He surprised me by telling me he wanted to give me some money to help cover the time I had been away from work. He said he thought his father would want him to do this. Right away, I said, "I didn't do this for money." That must have sounded really stupid, and

I don't know why I said it. He said, "I know that." I felt foolish. I told him it was a very sweet offer, and the subject was dropped. It was a very nice gesture, and it really helped. The trip had been a significant financial hit.

After breakfast, he walked me home and asked if I would like to join him the following day when he took his mom and sister across Hood Canal for lunch at my very favorite restaurant. He was planning to take them on a quick tour of a waterfront town that is really quite beautiful. He said I was welcome and that he would like the company. I said yes. To be honest, I kind of missed Joan. We had been inseparable for fourteen days, and I felt very protective of her. She always smiled when she saw me, and it was nice to know she still recognized me as someone familiar.

FIELD TRIP

I met Sean at his house Sunday morning. Joan and Ally were already there. Joan was walking around Sean's house looking at things and rearranging papers on his kitchen table. She looked happy to be out and about. I asked her if she was ready for a trip, and she said, "Who? Me? Well, let's go. Go, go, go." We all climbed into her car. She recognized the Wisconsin plates and said, "This is my car." It was something she did from the window of the ALF as well. She would point out her car.

It was a beautiful day, and there was an open table when we got to the restaurant. Joan was strategically placed in the corner where she would be boxed in, and Ally sat next to her. Sean was outside talking on the phone. A cousin had called from Wisconsin wanting details about a memorial service. Sean's list kept getting longer. By the time he joined us, Joan had peeled open most of the grape jellies and was sticky. Happy, but sticky. We had a wonderful breakfast and followed it with spectacular pie. The restaurant was known for its pies.

While we were talking, Ally thanked us for letting her sit facing the door. Sean asked why, and she said that all law enforcement liked to sit that way so they could see what was coming. Police officers had entered the restaurant, and that started the shift in conversation. She explained you were never off-duty when you were a cop. Sean asked what if they were coming from the kitchen, which she did not find funny. I did, though, and when I laughed Joan did as well.

Ally took bathroom duty with Joan, and we drove up to the waterfront. It was getting a little chilly in the breeze, and Joan kept saying how cold it was. Sean ended up buying her a man's jacket off a rack in front of a store. It fit her well, and she looked cute. We walked up and down the street window shopping and then watched the boats.

It was my turn for bathroom duty. Luckily for us, there were very nice public restrooms, and we went into the handicapped stall. I handed her one of the paper seat covers, and she put it over her head like a necklace. I started laughing and tried again. The third one made it to the toilet seat. She was not interested in wiping, but we got it done and went back into the sunshine. We knew she was ready to go when she started asking, "Is that my car?" as we walked past anything similar to hers. It was a nice day, and I enjoyed walking down the street holding hands with Joan.

We returned to Sean's house, and I said my good-byes. I went home and got myself ready for a return to a normal week. I got all of my errands and cleaning done and lined up my cases for the morning. I was going to try to take some time off from Joan, Sean, and his sister. I wanted to step back and let them make the decisions that needed to be made about services, finances, and Joan's care.

WEDNESDAY THE TENTH

I had been off duty for a week. I had slept in my own bed and woke up to the sound of my coffee maker every morning. I wish I could say I had jumped right back into work, but I hadn't. Something was different, and I was having a very hard time concentrating on work. It just didn't seem to matter.

I had a pile of cases waiting to be done, and I just couldn't pull myself together enough to fully engage. I found my thoughts wandering; I would read the same page over and over again and still not know what it said. I had a really big case that involved nursing home care, but I could not bring myself to even look at it. I simply did not want to work. I wanted to write this story.

I had avoided going to see Joan while Sean's sister was there. While our weekend field trip had gone reasonably well, I just didn't feel the need to spend time with her. We were not going to be friends, we didn't have to get along, and I wanted to steer clear. Her departure the following day meant Sean and I needed to work out a schedule, so we decided to get together for dinner.

Sean asked me if I wanted to pop in for just a minute to say good-bye to his sister. I reluctantly said okay, and we stopped at the ALF before going to dinner. I'm glad we did. I gave Ally my pair of jeweler's cutters so she could remove her mom's rings, and we sat down for a few minutes. She had taken her mom to a local doctor the memory care director had recommended, and both she and Joan had really liked him. Ally and Joan had done pretty well together.

When I got up to leave, I wished her well. She gave me a hug and thanked me for everything I had done for her family. She sounded sincere. I told her I was glad she had spent time with her mom. She said she really liked the area and planned on coming back. I think she had a much clearer picture of her mom's future. Ally was pleasant that evening, and I am glad I got to see that side of her.

Sean and I walked out together and headed to the restaurant. When we sat down, he told me he had gotten a call from someone in the corporate office of the ALF asking if he would consider the sister facility again since memory care was still full. It had just been a voice mail, but he was wondering if Joan was wearing out her welcome in memory care. He had to consider what to do if the wait for a bed was prolonged. We both needed to work, and trying to sleep in the ALF would make that very difficult.

We talked about various scenarios, and the possibility of looking into other facilities for a short-term placement was raised. We had looked at another facility before finding the ALF Joan was in, but it hadn't felt like a good fit. Sean wondered if he should take another look.

There was a third facility we had not visited, and we talked about maybe making some visits the following day. Sean had the day off because he had a morning appointment and then was going to take his sister to the airport. I said I would take the afternoon off if he wanted to look at the possible options.

We had a nice dinner and went our separate ways. I went to bed knowing that the next night would not be as peaceful. At this point, there was no end in sight, and I didn't know how much more I could give.

Thursday the Eleventh

Thursday morning, I woke with a plan. I decided to do some research on possible options and made some calls. I spoke with the other two ALFs in our town. Both had beds available. I had a much better idea of what Joan needed now and knew what to ask.

The first possibility was right up the street from my house. I am grateful for the honest feedback I got from their admissions director. When I explained that Joan needed both a locked unit and an environment that allowed for socialization with other residents, he was blunt. He said that if we were in an urgent situation, she could certainly be admitted to the locked unit, but that the overall function level of the current residents was significantly lower than what I had described as Joan's current state. He said the residents were all pretty far advanced and most did not talk or interact with others.

That was a concern Sean had voiced about the ill-fated sister facility, and I knew he would not be able to leave his mother in a place where he felt she would know she did not fit in. She was very cheerful and outgoing in her Alzheimer's, and we feared that if she were placed in an environment where she had no feedback or opportunities for friendship, she would regress or lose her amazingly upbeat personality.

The second possibility was the memory care unit we had looked at a few months earlier. It was much bigger than the twenty-four-bed unit Joan was waiting for, and on the day we had visited we saw almost no interaction between staff and residents, residents and residents, or even between staff. It felt cold and empty. It was a lovely setting with gorgeous views, but we didn't get a sense of warmth.

I called the admissions coordinator who had given us a tour after hosting us for lunch. She didn't remember us. I'm sure she meets lots of families who are looking for options and answers. I gave her an update on our situation and asked about vacancies. They had both a private and semiprivate room available: one on the floor for "pleasantly confused" residents and one on the floor for more impaired people.

I told her I would talk with Joan's son later that morning and call her back. I said we would be making a decision in a matter of days. She asked if she could fax admission orders to Joan's local doctor, and I said no. I was not making the decision; that would only be done after Sean had another look at the units. Something about her offer bothered me, but I am sure she was only trying to be helpful.

My next thought was to hire an in home-based caregiver to stay with Joan in the ALF at night. Sean was working in Seattle and took the 5:20 a.m. ferry every morning. Staying overnight with Joan would cost him at least three to four hours of work every day. He wouldn't be able to carpool, which would increase his commuting costs significantly. It went without saying that he would not get a decent night's sleep.

If I stayed with her, I would be faced with trying to do my job while exhausted. I didn't need lots of sleep, but getting up every night at 1:30 a.m. and then again at 4:00 a.m. really affects the quality of sleep. I have a newfound respect for both parents of infants and the thousands, if not millions, of people who care for family members at home. It is a full-time job that I know many, many people are doing on top of their regular jobs. It is exhausting because you are never "off duty."

I toyed with the idea of Sean and I doing a split shift where I would come over at 4:00 a.m. so he could go to work. That would work if I worked in the afternoon and evening. We could piece our time together to make sure she was never alone. It was far from a good solution, though, so I priced an in-home companion. The going rate was $23 per hour, with a three-hour minimum. That would be expensive on top of the monthly rent Joan was already paying at the ALF.

The last option I thought of was to try to hire someone through word of mouth. One of Sean's friends had a girlfriend who worked as an aide, so I thought maybe Sean could ask her for suggestions. He knew her pretty well. I found out later that she had offered to help.

OUT OF THE BLUE

Sean called me a little after noon. He had dropped Ally off at the airport and was driving home when he got a call from the ALF. A bed had opened in memory care. One of the residents had passed away, and Joan was going to get the space. It would be several days until she could move, but this was absolutely wonderful news that came out of the blue.

Joan was going to move into the unit where she was already known. We had been very happy with the staff and the environment of the memory care unit, and we were so grateful for the way the ALF had opened its doors to us and found a way to get us through these very stressful weeks.

I knew Sean would feel comfortable with his mom staying there and would know she was safe and well cared-for. This unit felt like a home. Things were going to work out, and his life as a single parent to his mother could start to normalize.

I was thrilled and invited him out to dinner to celebrate. There was a family grieving the loss of a parent, and while I offered prayers for them, I was simply overjoyed for Joan. That may sound callous, but it's the truth. We offered a quick prayer for the woman who had passed away and gave thanks that Joan would soon be home.

We did not know exactly when she would be moving, so we made short-term plans. I told him I would stay with Joan Thursday and Sunday so he could go to work. He was going to cover the weekend nights, and we would both have days off as Joan spent every day in memory care.

As we waited for dinner to come, I asked Sean if he had been getting calls from his friends. He said, "A few." I asked if the people in AA knew what he had been going through and he said, "Some do." I was still dismayed by what I saw as a total lack of support from his village. I asked him if he had reached out for any kind of help, and he said he "didn't like people knowing his business." I completely understood the desire for privacy but wondered if he had purposefully kept his village away, deciding that as long as I was there, no other help was needed.

I added that to my list of things I needed to think about. In our time as a couple, it seemed like the more I gave, the less he gave in return. That was my fault as much as his. I continued to give, and it became an increasingly unequal partnership. Would our new chapter be any different? These questions ran through my mind as we sat on a waterfront deck and munched on happy hour specials.

Sean asked how I was doing on the book. I had told him I wanted to write one before his last trip to Wisconsin. I had joked about calling it *The Long, Long, Long Way Home*. When I decided I really was going to write a book, I asked how he felt about it, and he was very supportive, encouraging me to follow my heart. He thought it was a good idea, and so had the people he mentioned it to.

When he asked about it, I told him I was already working on it and would like to hear some of his impressions of the trip. He thought for a minute and then said he did not remember much of it—not specifics. His most prominent memory was the feeling of being in the car that had become our own private universe. It had been surreal to be traveling down the road knowing that the cars going by had no idea we were in a life-and-death struggle. It was just the four of us. I understood exactly what he was saying.

After our early dinner, he went to pick up Joan, and I went home and packed a bag. I made a few phone calls, sharing the news that soon Joan would be moving into memory care and I would be home full time. I knew that once she was settled, it would be the start of a new chapter in my life. Sean and I would not be as intertwined. Much of what had kept us closely bound over the last six months were his parents. Now it would be time to move on and see if we could sustain a friendship.

Sean texted me that his mom's wedding band was missing. His sister had cut off the engagement ring the night before but had left her band in place. I had tried unsuccessfully to remove it several times before as we tried to swap out her real jewelry for fabulous fakes I had acquired through the Home Shopping Network. I had rings I didn't wear, and we wanted to keep her jewelry safe. Somehow she had managed to get that band off during the day, and it was nowhere to be found.

I signed back into the ALF at the front desk and went to the apartment. I thought Sean should be the one to go to the memory care unit and ask them to keep an eye out for the ring. Joan gave me a big smile and waved her fingers at me. She was wearing the rings I had put in her jewelry case. The wedding band is still lost somewhere in the ALF, but it wasn't the fault of anyone other than us. Joan doesn't miss it.

Sean went home, and Joan and I were once again on the prowl for entertainment. We went to the lobby to look at the mountains and then walked outside to smell the flowers. She pointed out the two dead trees across the parking lot and said they were too big and really messy. "Someone should fix'em, clean it up, you know, sweep or something." We looked at the cars, and she did not see hers. She asked where her car was and accepted my answer that her son had it and was going to give it a bath to try to get rid of the cigarette odor. She wrinkled her nose when I said cigarettes and said, "Yuck, yuck, ishhhhh." I agreed.

We had a quiet evening. We watched *Wipeout* on TV, and she found it to be very funny when people got knocked into the water. I called Sean so he could hear her laugh. She got ready for bed without any problems and took her pills on the fourth attempt. I decided to use the TV as a nightlight. I left it on with the volume turned off so it would illuminate the living room. I thought it might make it easier for her to see where she was when she got up during the night.

It was the best night we had, and she only got up twice. Right on schedule at 1:40 a.m. and again at 4:05 a.m. Both trips to the bathroom were pretty uneventful, and we both slept until almost 7:00 a.m. Friday morning.

FRIDAY THE TWELFTH

Friday felt almost normal. I dropped Joan off at memory care and went home to shower. I was focused enough to get quite a bit of work done before meeting a client for lunch. This was the same client I had seen the day Henry died, and he asked how we were doing. He had recently started dealing with questions of cognitive issues with his mother, and we had discussed these types of topics before.

We talked about his mom, Henry, Joan, and what it was like to live in an ALF at the ripe old age of forty-seven. For the first time, I decided to join my client in a glass of wine with lunch. I usually stick with coffee, but his glass looked very tempting, and I joined him. It was just the one glass, but when I got home I started giggling and couldn't stop. I guess I needed a laugh.

I ignored my phone when it rang because I knew I would laugh at whoever was calling. It was Sean, and when he called back a few minutes later, I was still laughing. He asked if I would be okay to drive later that afternoon—he needed a ride to pick up his van. I was done giggling by the end of business and followed him in his mom's car. When we got back to the ALF, we picked up Joan and took her to the Burger King drive-through. We had a little picnic in her apartment, and then I went home.

I spent the rest of the evening rearranging my desk and putting cases in the order in which they had to be done. I was pushing some deadlines and was far from caught up. I once again told myself I would get started in the morning and wondered why I was so apathetic about working. I just could not get my mind focused on my work, but I knew I needed to get over it and get to work. Tomorrow…I would do better tomorrow.

THE WEEKEND

Saturday came and went, and we still didn't know when Joan could move. We had learned that the single room was being held while a family of one of the current residents decided if they wanted to move their mother out of a semiprivate room. If they decided to move her, Joan would get a semiprivate space, and if they decided against a move she would get the private room. I can't speak for Sean, but I did not care one way or the other.

Early in the day, I stopped by Sean's house to help him unpack the cube, which he had picked up after many miscommunications and phone calls. It was sad to see some of the things Henry had wanted us to bring. Sean was going to donate all of his clothing, and I put it right into the trunk of their car. We got everything out of the cube pretty quickly. Sean left with a friend to return the cube, and I kept sorting. I put together a bag of things to take when Joan moved into the memory care unit.

I separated the costume jewelry from anything valuable. The "good stuff" would be kept in a safe. The costume jewelry would be brought to Joan in small batches so she had things to enjoy and share with her friends. If it got lost, it would not matter. I left in the early afternoon and ran a few errands. I was feeling restless.

I met Sean and Joan that evening at the market, and we got slices of pizza. Joan had a little bit of trouble eating as there were many distractions. She kept wanting to open straws and dispose of the wrappers. We did not stay long, but it was a Saturday night I will remember. We walked around the market looking at cookies, the deli counter, the cheese selection, etc. They had ice cream cups on sale at ten for $10, and Sean loaded up. Her apartment had a kitchenette, and the freezer was pretty much empty. We went back to her apartment and put some ice cream on the counter to soften.

Then it happened. Joan released a stink bomb. She had been displaying some pretty impressive gas since our arrival in

Washington. She never closed the bathroom door, so everyone in the apartment was privy to her gas. It gave us more than a few laughs. On this evening, though, it was no laughing matter. We heard it, and it just kept coming. I walked over to check on her and walked into a wall of stink. It was horrible.

I walked back toward Sean with a look on my face that got his attention. A few seconds later, he smelled it. It was everywhere. We put the ice cream away, and I went hunting for air freshener. I looked in the laundry room, in the community kitchen, and in every possible cabinet in the apartment. I came up empty, and it was getting worse.

I was lucky it was Sean's night. I told him it was time for me to head out and laughed at his response. As I was walking down to my car, I remembered that I had a small bottle of Febreze in my glove compartment. I was almost to my car when I heard a soft "Help me." I looked up to see that Sean had plastered himself to the living room window as he breathed fresh air. I told him to hold on a minute and found the spray. I held it up and asked if he wanted it. He said, "I'll be right down." I was glad he was the one going back to the apartment.

WHAT DO I DO?

Sean had an interesting evening with his mother, and he wasn't sure what to do if it happened again. It was clear that Joan really liked him. Sean's sister had joked that Joan had a crush on him. She called him the cute boy, cutie, sweetie, and always lit up when he hugged her. It was also clear that she rarely knew he was her son. He was mostly the cute boy who visited her and she liked.

He told me that when it was time for bed, his mom was kind of flirting with him. When he went to turn down the sheets for her, she told him which side of the bed was his. He was really shocked when she said, "We don't have to do anything crazy." He told me that he said, "This is your bed, MOM. My bed is out there." It was a new twist in our ever-changing experience. It started to make sense the next day, but it must have been really uncomfortable for Sean when it happened.

RESTLESS IN THE ALF

Sunday passed without an answer, so I packed a bag and went back to the ALF. I picked Joan up from memory care and asked if they had heard anything. The weekend staff had nothing to do with it, but they said it couldn't be much longer. They had expected her to move over the weekend. I guess the other family was still thinking. Joan was pacing when I found her. She looked restless and was speaking in fragments I couldn't follow. I thought I would try the old ice cream diversion, and we went for a walk.

We went down to the dining room, and I made a cone for each of us. It was the first time she had difficulty eating it. It was melting down the sides, but she kept licking the top of it and letting it run down her hands. She would not sit down so we just kept moving.

We were down to the bottom of the cones when we got to her apartment. She did not like the bottom of the cone, the flat part on the very bottom. She did not eat it but tended to hang onto it until she decided what to do. I had found them on the end table, in the bathroom, and once in the toilet—but she held onto this one for awhile.

I sent Sean a text: "I have yet to understand our conversation. Very scattered."

He called me, thinking I was talking about him, not his mother. He asked what I was confused about. I thought that was funny. We chatted for a minute and agreed we would cross our fingers for a decision in the morning. My attention had been focused on Sean, and when I got off the phone the cone bottom was gone. It was a mystery.

It took me almost an hour to get her into her PJs and ready for bed. We had a great deal of difficulty in the bathroom. She could not grasp the concept of toilet paper. She put some in the trash can, put some on the floor, and draped the handrail with it. Wiping was quite a project that evening. Pills were equally challenging. By 9:00 p.m., I was exhausted.

I put her music on and hoped for the best. I walked out of her room to get her and found her climbing into my bed by the door. I redirected her to her room and pulled back the sheets. That was something I did every night. I pulled the sheets back and held them while she climbed in. I would then cover her up and wish her a good night's sleep. It was the routine we were used to.

She didn't lie down, though. She slid over so there was room for me and said, "Aren't you getting in?" I wasn't surprised by that, given Sean's story from the night before. I told her I would stay with her until she fell asleep and lay down on top of the covers. That satisfied her, and she went right to sleep.

I think she was showing us that she knew something was different. She had noticed she was sleeping alone, and that wasn't normal. She had not mentioned Henry since he left for hospice and did not know he had died. Sean was trying to decide how to approach that conversation, but so far she hadn't asked. It is my opinion that it was Henry's absence that caused these changes in her. She was reacting to something but didn't know what.

She was up at 1:12 a.m., and after using the bathroom, she tried to get into the twin bed with me. I led her back to the bedroom and turned on her CD. I stayed with her until she went to sleep.

Smells Good but Doesn't Work that Well

I woke to the sound of an aerosol spray. I looked over into the bathroom, but it was dark and empty. I looked up at the microwave; it was 4:47 a.m. I could not place the source of the spraying. I sat up and saw Joan.

She was standing in front of the TV. It was on with no sound. She was standing about a foot in front of it and spraying her hair with vigor. I jumped up and ran over. I was hit by a wall of apple cinnamon. It was the air freshener Sean had given me the day before in case of another "incident." I had put it in the bathroom cabinet.

She had found it and was using it as hair spray. Her hair was soaked. It appeared she might have used it as deodorant as well, for her night gown was heavily scented. I took her hand and released the spray. I said, "This is not hair spray, Joan. I think we can put it away now." She looked at me like I was crazy and pointed to the can. "Hair spray. Hair spray." She shook her hair in my face and said, "Doesn't it smell good?" I had to agree—it smelled great. The can actually said, "Air spray," but at 4:47 a.m. it really didn't matter.

The problem with using air freshener as hair spray is that it was quite sticky, very runny, and not at all conducive to styling. I decided it was time to start our day and suggested that a shower would be a good idea. She seemed okay with idea so we headed into the bathroom. I distracted her with her toothbrush and tooth paste while I grabbed towels and the shower supplies. I pulled down the shower chair, which was mounted on the shower wall and could be folded up when not in use.

I got her started in the shower and quickly laid my clothes out on the bed by the door. I knew I was going to have to get dressed quickly because Joan was up for the day. I was trying to save time. When I walked back in the bathroom, I got a surprise. Joan had used the shower chair as a toilet and was trying to clean the seat with her hands. I stepped into the shower with her and got her cleaned up. I turned off the water and moved her out onto the bathroom floor to dry off. I handed her a towel, and she started drying her toes.

I turned back to the shower, which needed a good cleaning. As I focused on the shower stall, she walked out of the bathroom, picked up my pants, and put them on. She then walked back into the bathroom, sat on the toilet, and pooped. Unfortunately, she had not pulled down my pants, and I realized I was going home in my pajamas. It happened in less than a minute. She was organized and deliberate in getting those pants on while I was cleaning the shower.

We got the pants off, and she continued to use the toilet. When it was time to wipe, I folded the squares for her as she liked them and handed her the first one. She promptly used it to towel dry her hair and then put it in the toilet. The squares actually used for wiping were put on the bathroom counter. We were not having a good day.

The shower was now clean, so Joan went in for round two, and I bagged and disposed of my pants, accepting that sometimes it is best to just throw it away. The shower went smoothly, and she dried off without incident. I got her dressed and sat her down in a chair to put on her shoes and socks. As she worked on this task, I texted her son.

"Damn that air spray. Mom just used as hair spray. F—ing mess. Also pooped in my pants. She did, not me."

That resulted in an immediate call back. "I'm really sorry, so sorry." He wasn't the one who pooped in my pants, but he certainly felt bad about the morning we were having.

He was already at work. I felt like I was, too. I was very appreciative of the kind staff person who took her down to memory care so I did not have to show the world my PJs. I hurried out to my car, and I think only a handful of people saw my star-covered ensemble. I started a big pot of coffee and took a really long, hot shower.

PLEASE LET IT BE TODAY

It goes without saying that I was a little frazzled. Work was not going very well, and I was nearing the end of my willingness or ability to do this. It had been twenty-six days since I flew to Wisconsin.

When I agreed to help Sean, this was not what either of us had in mind. He had no way of knowing his father would barely make it to Washington. We had not given a thought to the lack of a bed in memory care since his parents were going to live together in the apartment. What we signed up for and the scenario we had actually faced were two completely different situations.

My friend Louise had been shocked to hear that I went to Wisconsin. She had been my confidant as I decided I needed to move out of the house I shared with Sean and knew of my very complicated feelings about him. Her text, once she knew what I was doing, was, "You are a far better woman than I. God Bless you."

My sister's response had been "Holy cow!" followed shortly by, "Oh my goodness. Thoughts, prayers, and hugs to you."

My parents had not been surprised by my decision to go, but they worried about how much of myself I was giving away. They were sending cards, care packages, and even flowers while Sean and I shared custody of Joan. Sean said, "I should be the one sending you flowers," when he saw the beautiful arrangement my parents had sent. I agreed.

The overall consensus was that it had been the right thing to do, but there had to be a limit to how much I could give for the man I was no longer involved with. He had told me he did not want to be in a committed relationship with me, but our current relationship seemed much deeper than all of the things he didn't want.

When I left the ALF in my PJs, I was praying that a bed would open. It was time to move into our next chapter, and I was ready to redefine the lines. It was not to be, though. At noon I got a call from

Robert, saying he was hopeful the move could take place on Tuesday. Twenty-four more hours...

I called Sean to let him know about the call, and there was an obvious hesitancy on his end of the line as he said, "So tonight...?" and trailed off into silence. I dug deep into my heart and told him I had one more night left in me and would relieve him by 8:00 p.m. He would pick her up and spend the evening with her until I got there. One more night—I could do anything for one more night.

ONE MORE NIGHT

I walked into Joan's apartment expecting the worst, and once again I was wrong. She was smiling when I saw her and gave me a big hug. It was a total change from the night before. We sat on the couch and chatted for a while. Most of the time, I was unsure of the topic, but we were communicating, and she seemed much calmer.

After Sean left, Joan and I walked down to visit with Renee, the community relations director. She had been the one to show Sean and me around several months before, and she was one of those people you liked as soon as you met her. She was deeply committed to her job and loved the residents. They could feel it, and she got lots of hugs.

I wanted to thank her for everything that had been done for us. I know she played a large role in working out a solution that allowed Joan to stay until a bed opened. Joan liked her, too. Joan gave her a huge smile and a pat on the shoulder, then walked out of her office to examine the bookshelves one book at a time. She would read the title and author out loud and move the book to a different shelf. I knew I had a few minutes to talk with Renee.

Renee asked how we were doing. I had her laughing really hard when I told her about the apple cinnamon incident. She had a grandmother who had traveled Joan's path, and we had talked about that before, about the different ways people manifest this terrible and unfair disease. Joan was very fortunate in her happiness and positive personality. We both hoped she would be able to keep her joy as things progressed.

When Joan was done with the books, we returned to our room, had some ice cream, and called it a night. Aside from her two usual trips to the bathroom, she slept well, and so did I. I was awake and on my second cup of coffee when a text arrived at 6:39 a.m.

"How did it go and how is it going?"

I answered, "No poop. Getting dressed, doing better."

"Good deal ☺"

It was shower time, and we did well. She got dressed by herself and only needed help with her shoelaces, which she had managed to knot about ten times on each side. It took a while, but she was patient and looked at Ronald while I untangled the laces. I dropped her off at 7:29 a.m. and went back to her apartment.

I silently willed the other family to make a decision, and I packed the apartment in about ten minutes. She didn't have all that much stuff, and I lined everything up by the door, stripped the beds, and packed my things.

Right before I left, I felt a stabbing pain in my right temple and knew what was coming. I had severe headaches after an accident in 2008 and this was how they started. I reached into my purse to get some Tylenol and felt something mushy. I looked in and there was the bottom of Joan's ice cream cone. I had been carrying it around since Sunday night.

I sent a text saying, "Totally packed, hope you get the call. I have first migraine since moved to Washington. Going to bed." I did exactly that.

THE CALL WE WERE WAITING FOR

At a little after 3:00 p.m., Sean called. The other family had turned down the private room, and it was being cleaned for Joan. She could move within the hour. I told him I would be there in ten minutes. It actually took me about twelve.

When I walked in the door, Renee was at the reception desk. She looked over at me, smiled, and said, "Hurray." She offered to help me pack, and I told her it was already done. She said she would help me move and we went upstairs. We grabbed a laundry cart out of the laundry room and loaded it up. I pulled the big rolling suitcase and the memory foam mattress topper, and we made it in one trip.

Renee helped me unpack, and the maintenance man brought in and assembled the bed. I had all of her linens waiting, and we put together a very well-coordinated bedroom ensemble. I had picked out gold and burgundy linens. Joan had a huge pillowcase embroidered with her name on it, which I had used for the color palette. I thought that would be helpful in getting her used to her new room.

The room was really nice, and we were settled in in less than fifteen minutes. All of her clothes were labeled, and I had scattered her picture books and photos around the room. I had, of course, given Ronald Reagan a place of importance on her nightstand. He had been my friend throughout the trip, and I knew he would help Joan recognize the space as hers.

Renee told me she thought Sean was lucky to have a friend like me, and without really thinking I said "You don't know the half of it, Renee."

"What do you mean?"

"The part you don't know is that Sean and I broke up a few months ago. We lived together for twenty months, and I just moved out in April. This all started happening while we were separating."

Renee looked shocked. "Are you kidding me? You broke up and *then* you decided to help him move his parents and live here with them?"

"I know."

"It's okay to take care of yourself now. You know it's time, right? You deserve to be happy. You have gone far above and beyond, and you have done right by his parents."

We hugged and I thanked her. She was an amazing woman, and I was grateful to have met her.

After Renee left, I let Sean know Joan had moved and gave him the room number. I said we could both go to our own homes and relax tonight. He texted back, saying he was "Waiting on a view of the back of our eyelids." It would be the first night either of us would go to bed knowing that the following day would bring more stability than the day before. Life would never be the same as it was three and a half weeks ago, but at least we could both start to find our new normal.

I brought Joan into the room and showed her the pictures of her parents and sister. She moved a few things around and went back into the common space. It was an easy transition for her. She liked it there. A few days before, she had given Sean and me a description of the unit that I found to be so very endearing.

When I asked if she liked it there, she replied it was "a nice little town. You don't have to walk far to the store, and there is a restaurant right down the street." We asked if her neighbors were nice, and she smiled and said, "Good people." I had to agree with her assessment, as I really liked her "town," too.

I left a little before 5 p.m., after getting Joan settled into her seat in the "restaurant." I walked to my car knowing that Joan was safe, comfortable, and surrounded by people who would love her.

It was Tuesday, August 16. It had been twenty-four days since we pulled out of their driveway in Wisconsin. It had been an extremely raw and incredibly exhausting journey, but Sean and I had pulled together and accomplished what we set out to do. We had brought his father to Washington and settled his mother into her next chapter.

Tonight, we would all be home.

EPILOGUE

When Joan moved into the memory care unit, there were the expected bumps as the unit got used to her and we got used to the unit. I dropped in frequently to see how she was doing. Sean and I rarely went together. I went during the day, and he visited after work and on the weekends. It worked well for us.

I remained a bit of a mystery to the staff because I was not family in the legal sense. Some thought Sean and I were married, and some thought I was Joan's daughter. Sean always introduced me as his best friend. I found that saying she was my second mom worked well and I was really glad they took the time to ask. It was wonderful that they knew who was walking in the door.

I was thrilled it had worked out so well for both Joan and Sean. Having his mom close by in a loving environment was a relief as he faced what became his new "normal." There was much left to be done, but at least he could be exhausted and overwhelmed in the comfort of his own home.

Henry's decision to retain both control and access to his finances created a big job for Sean. He spent a great deal of time hunting down information on pensions, policies, and accounts. All of that could have been done ahead of time if Henry had been willing to help. There is still much left to do in getting Henry and Joan's affairs in order.

Joan started asking where her husband was. We told her once that he had passed away and was in heaven, but the answer did not register. She sometimes wanted to call him to say she would be late getting home and worried about driving herself at night. We told her that we would take her anywhere she needed to go. The subject was only briefly upsetting to her and quickly forgotten. Like my grandmother had done, Joan took to calling herself by her maiden name.

The philosophy of this unit was that we should take Joan's journey with her. If she thought Henry was alive, we did not correct her. If she was young and her daddy was coming to visit, then we were happy he was coming. If wearing all of her jewelry at once seemed like a good idea, who were we to say anything about it? Shoelaces were an unnecessary complication, so slip-on shoes became the norm. We wanted her to be happy, and because she would never return to our reality, it was up to us to enjoy hers.

Alzheimer's is unrelenting in its cruelness, and as I finish writing this book, Joan no longer recognizes me. The last flicker of recognition I got from her was on her eightieth birthday in early October. I stopped by in the morning to decorate her room. She smiled when she saw me coming, and I knew I was familiar. Sean and I brought cupcakes for all of the residents at dinner. When we lit the candle on her cupcake and sang to her, she was not able to blow out the candle. She didn't know what to do. Sean was heartbroken.

As for me and Sean, we found our own new "normal," settling into a close friendship with clear boundaries and far less intertwined lives. Recognizing that we are not suited as a couple has made it so much easier to appreciate the friend I used to have. For the first time ever, we are equal in what we want. There are no more "what ifs," and no lingering thoughts of "if only" things had been different.

Shortly after Joan moved into memory care, he sent me a text saying, "I haven't expressed how profoundly grateful I am for your friendship. There have been times that without you I'd surely be lost. Thank you."

My answer was, "There is no man that has been a more important part of my life. You are my history and my best friend." With apologies to my father, who played a central role in my life and is in a category of his own, this statement was true. Sean changed the course of my life several times over a thirty-year period.

Without our friendship, my life would have gone in a different direction. I would not have moved to Texas and met my friend Louise, who is as easily entertained by the little things in life as I am.

I also would not have moved to Washington, where I went back to camp and rediscovered my love of developmentally disabled adults.

I believe that everything happens for a reason. People cross paths because they are meant to. Believing this has helped me understand why I came to Washington. Sean and I crossed paths again because we needed each other. He gave me peace, comfortable silence, and passion when my life in Florida was filled with chaos, drama, and pain. I gave him a solid foundation when he decided to land and live a sober life.

I have come to believe that we re-entered each other's lives because we were meant to take this journey together. In the time Sean and I lived together he was, without knowing it, preparing for this enormous responsibility. He became financially responsible and left old habits behind. I like to think I helped him with that, but he made the changes. At the same time, Sean showed me very clearly that what I need and want in a committed relationship was not to be found with him. Because of Sean, my life will once again undergo major changes.

I was very far away from my own family, and that was something I vowed to change. Shortly after this story ended, I moved to North Carolina, where I hoped to find a way to combine my love for working with developmentally disabled adults with my work as a nurse consultant. Once I settled back into my life, I was able to refocus my attention on my work, and found I still enjoyed it. Very much.

I have already had a frank discussion with my parents about what they want to have happen when the time comes. Luckily for me, they have always been open to discussing these types of subjects. I know what they want and will honor their wishes. My mom and I have joked for years that when her time is near, I should make cookies and hot chocolate, loosen the porch railings, and then show her the spectacular mountain views from their deck. In all honesty, it doesn't sound like a bad way to go.

I am determined that I will have my affairs in order long before it is a necessity and have already updated my will and power of attorney forms. I have talked with my brothers and sister about doing the same. I am also determined that I will not let material possessions replace what is truly important. Things are just things. I want to focus on what really matters and what is important to me. Thankfully, I have figured out what that is.

As people came to learn about our trip, the question I was asked repeatedly was "Why did you do it? Why did you do that for the man who broke your heart?"

My answer is that I did not do it for the forty-eight-year-old man I could not understand. I did it for the eighteen-year-old boy who stole my heart with a poem. I did it for Joan and Henry, who were my second parents and welcomed me into their home and lives. I did it because my parents raised me to believe I could do anything if I set my mind to it. I did it because I could.

Most of all, however, I did it for me. Because I am clear in what type of person I want to be: A woman who can do the right thing even when it is difficult. A woman who will not let someone else's vision of her cloud her own. The result of taking this extraordinary journey was that I was given something priceless: a clean slate.

I am intent on finding and sharing joy. Joy in my work, in my life, and if I am lucky, with a partner who will judge me by my character, actions, and heart. I hope to be a better daughter, sister, aunt, nurse, and friend. I will start by being a better version of myself. I left Washington with no regrets and no questions in my mind about what might have been. I am completely free, and I am sure I am headed in the right direction.

When I was in sixth grade, I wrote my first novel. I worked on it during lunch and passed the pages to my friends as I wrote them. I still have that book, and having recently read it, I truly hope my writing skills have improved. Through the years, I have found myself thinking about writing a book, but it wasn't until we pulled in to see Crazy Horse that I knew I was *supposed* to write one.

As I settled into my new home, I once again hung my poem on the wall. When I look at it now, I will do so with the newfound appreciation of what these lines mean:

Through our hearts we learn to love,
we learn to live and grow,
so please don't leave my heart behind
for the love I did not show

I opened my heart to Sean thirty years ago and have no regrets. No one will ever take his place in my heart, and a part of him is mine and mine alone. We love each other very much, but it is a love that can only be based in friendship.

No one has been left behind. He will always be with me, and we will celebrate each other's joys and share each other's sorrows. We are, finally, exactly where we should be.

The journey I took with Sean, Joan, and Henry gave me the gift of a fresh start. Thank you, Henry. Thank you, Joan.

And to Sean…I love you.

ACKNOWLEDGMENTS

First of all, I want to thank Sean for giving me his blessing in telling our story. This book would not have been published without it.

To Stephanie, whose friendship (and shoulder) was an unexpected gift that came out of my move to Washington. To Lyn, who has shown me unconditional love for as long as I can remember. To Julie, a wonderful mother with a beautiful heart.

To my two brothers—I love you. Go Bears!

To the campers and families who have allowed me to be a part of their lives—it is a privilege I treasure. To clients who have become friends—I know how very fortunate I am.

To my editor, Jon VanZile, whose pointed questions, honest feedback, and constant encouragement gave me the courage to tell the whole story. He shaped my words thoughtfully, showing me how to be a better writer.

And, finally, to Mom and Dad, whose love and unwavering support built the invisible cushion I always know is there. You have my respect, admiration, gratitude, and love.

CPSIA information can be obtained at www.ICGtesting.com
Printed in the USA
BVOW070739050412

286929BV00001B/2/P